DOWN BUT NOT OUT

Gritty Comebacks of India's Diehard Founders

DOWN BUT NOT OUT

Gritty Comebacks of India's Diehard Founders

SUBRATA MITRA

PANKAJ MISHRA

HARPER
BUSINESS

An Imprint of HarperCollins *Publishers*

First published in India by Harper Business 2026
An imprint of HarperCollins *Publishers*
HarperCollins *Publishers* India, Cyber City,
Building 10-A, Gurugram, Haryana – 122002, India
www.harpercollins.co.in

2 4 6 8 10 9 7 5 3 1

HB-ISBN: 978-93-6569-335-5
PB-ISBN: 978-93-7307-530-3
E-ISBN: 978-93-6569-244-0

Printed and bound at
Nutech Print Services Pvt. Ltd.

HarperCollins *Publishers*, Macken House, 39/40 Mayor Street Upper,
Dublin 1, D01 C9W8, Ireland

STILL HERE

Entrepreneurship is a trapeze act.

I know because I grew up watching it in the circus tents that came through town. The ground was always covered with sawdust, the drums built faster, as if they too were holding their breath.

High above, the trapeze artists would climb the ladder, their bodies outlined against the canvas roof. There was no safety net, only a crowd craning its necks upward. One would swing, legs cutting through the air. Then the moment would come. They would let go.

For a second too long, the body just hung there, between one bar and the other, between flight and fall.

Sometimes the hands met. The tent burst with claps and whistles. Sometimes they missed.

That's what entrepreneurship feels like. The ground below is unforgiving. And still, you leap. Sometimes you miss. Sometimes you are caught. Sometimes you keep flying, scarred but still moving.

Entrepreneurship is letting go before you know if anyone will catch you.

That is what this book is about.

Ben Horowitz once wrote about The Struggle: "The Struggle is when food loses its taste. The Struggle is when you are surrounded by people and you are all alone. The Struggle has no mercy. The Struggle is when you go on vacation to feel better and you feel worse."

I know that feeling. For me, it was FactorDaily. We set out to build a profitable, sustainable newsroom within three years. At the end of those three years, we hadn't. Then I came back and rebuilt FactorDaily as a nonprofit.

Entrepreneurship is a self-purification process – something redBus founder Phanindra Sama once told me on the *Outliers* podcast, and I remembered it then.

Entrepreneurship here also has its own metaphors. Subrata Mitra told me about ganna juice in India: the vendor doesn't throw away the cane after the first press. He twists it, feeds it back in, again and again, until one more trickle comes out. Bitter, but still juice.

Two decades ago, when Subrata or Sanjay Nayak first stepped out as entrepreneurs, the trapeze felt lonelier. The tent was half-empty, the lights dim, the swings fewer, the crowd unsure it even wanted to watch. India in the late 1990s and early 2000s was only just opening to a different kind of risk. Fewer than fifty million Indians had ever been online. Broadband meant dial-up whines, pages that loaded line by line. Building a startup here seemed eccentric, almost misplaced.

Over the past two decades, the lives of India's first 100-200 million urban internet users have been reshaped, bit by bit, by venture-backed companies. Ordering breakfast. Getting dressed for work. Calling a cab or a bike. Paying by UPI. Picking groceries. Buying jewelry. Selling a used car. Finding a haircut. Opening a demat account. Even the way we connect to the internet itself. What was once scattered, inconvenient, or out of reach is now stitched into daily habit.

For Subrata, there is quiet joy in having spent these twenty years close to that transformation – watching, and sometimes shaping, the outcomes across so many of these categories. This book gathers a set of founders who built those shifts from the inside. Their stories may not yet be widely known, but their work is already in the fabric of everyday life.

And then the ground shifted. By 2010, more than a hundred million Indians were connected. A decade later, that number had swelled to over seven hundred and fifty million, and today it is close to a billion. The fall in data costs after 2016 – among the cheapest anywhere in the world – meant the internet was no longer a privilege of offices and cities but something carried in pockets across villages. UPI stitched payments into everyday life; Aadhaar and cheap KYC gave rails for identity; smartphones dropped from luxury objects to household tools.

That was the tipping point. Flipkart could sell books out of a Bangalore apartment. BookMyShow could turn a movie ticket into a click. MakeMyTrip could shrink the travel agent's desk into a screen. The trapeze itself had not changed – but suddenly the tent was full, the lights brighter, the leap less invisible. India had become a founder ground.

A few years ago, in Coonoor, in one of my endless huddles with Avinash Raghava, he asked: Why don't you co-author a book with Subrata Mitra – one that tells the most raw, honest stories of entrepreneurs like never before?

Subrata had lived through his own failures. Founders trusted him because he carried those scars into every room. Avinash had already started Phoenix, a cohort for failed founders – not to help them get funded, but to help them rebuild resilience. Subrata agreed to be a coach. Watching him, I realized something I had missed even after building and failing myself: entrepreneurship is not something you own. It flows. Sometimes it crushes you. Sometimes it remakes you. Always, it tests who you are when nothing is left.

That was the seed of this book.

But seeds don't grow without soil. For me, that soil was Avinash Raghava. He prefers the background. In a world that rewards noise, Avinash has built his influence out of silence. Yet everywhere you look in India's entrepreneurial fabric, his fingerprints are there.

It was the same with this book. He kept shaping conversations without owning them, making space for founders to tell stories that might otherwise have stayed buried.

In every story here, family runs like an invisible current. Parents who left home to save, mothers who turned scarcity into learning, grandparents who filled gaps no one else could, spouses who absorbed the storms, children who waited, watched, and believed. Around them stood co-founders and first employees who staked their own futures on the same fragile idea. The founders may have taken the leap, but it was these hands that kept them from falling.

At first we thought it would be a 75,000-word book. We did the interviews, the reconstructions. But one day I asked: who reads 75,000 words today?

So we pivoted. Rajesh Subramanian, my FactorDaily colleague and friend, sketched chapters as a graphic novel. The founders loved it. We thought we had the answer.

We didn't.

Two or three chapters in, founders pushed back: You skipped the moment that broke me. Where is the raw truth?

So we pivoted again. Subrata scribbled names one afternoon, and the hybrid chapter was born – illustrations plus essay-lets. This time it fit. Founders laughed: Now you are pivoting like us.

And so this book became its own entrepreneurial journey.

Two years of long sessions with Subrata and Avinash. Subrata made time he didn't have, even after hospital visits and other commitments. Avinash flew in from Delhi and back at night several times. Me riding shotgun in Subrata's Porsche near Nandi Hills, conversations that wandered everywhere.

What I carry most is gratitude. For founders who spoke their hardest truths, and for Subrata and Avinash, who reminded me that entrepreneurship, for all its loneliness, is never a solo act.

I also want to acknowledge a few people without whom this book would not have taken the shape it has.

Rishi Dogra at Accel – for his deep listening, and for pushing the boundaries of creativity without ever making it feel intrusive.

Anish Chandy and the team at HarperCollins – for turning this project around.

Jayadevan PK for staying through the night proofreading the printed chapters.

And above all, the founders and their families – for opening their homes, and for all the chai, coffee, and food they fed me while I kept pressing them for more.

Pankaj Mishra

THE JOURNEYS

How to Read This Book

This isn't a manual or a playbook. It's not even a complete story.
What you hold in your hands is a set of lives, opened up in fragments. Some drawn, some written.

To read it well, a few reminders:

Read the pauses, not just the panels: The white space between two frames often carries more truth than the dialogue inside them.

What is unsaid matters: Founders often hold back more than they reveal. Look for the silences, the hesitations, the eyes that turn away.

Don't rush: These are not stories to be skimmed. Sit with one essay-let, one image. Let it linger.

See the contradictions: A celebrated exit that feels like failure. A shutdown that feels like survival. Both can be true at once.

Respect the ordinary: A line about five rupees, a child pressing a ten-rupee note into a mother's palm – these are not minor details. They are the marrow.

Feel before you analyze: Strategy will come later. First, allow the weight of what's human: the exhaustion, the humor, the doubt, the grace.

Remember – not-out: Every founder here carries a scar tissue. Some wins are unfinished, some losses never closed. That's the point.

01

THE PURSUIT OF TRUTH AND LONG-TERM GREED

A founder among founders: Subrata Mitra on carrying failure, backing others, and choosing the long game

To the One Still at the Crease

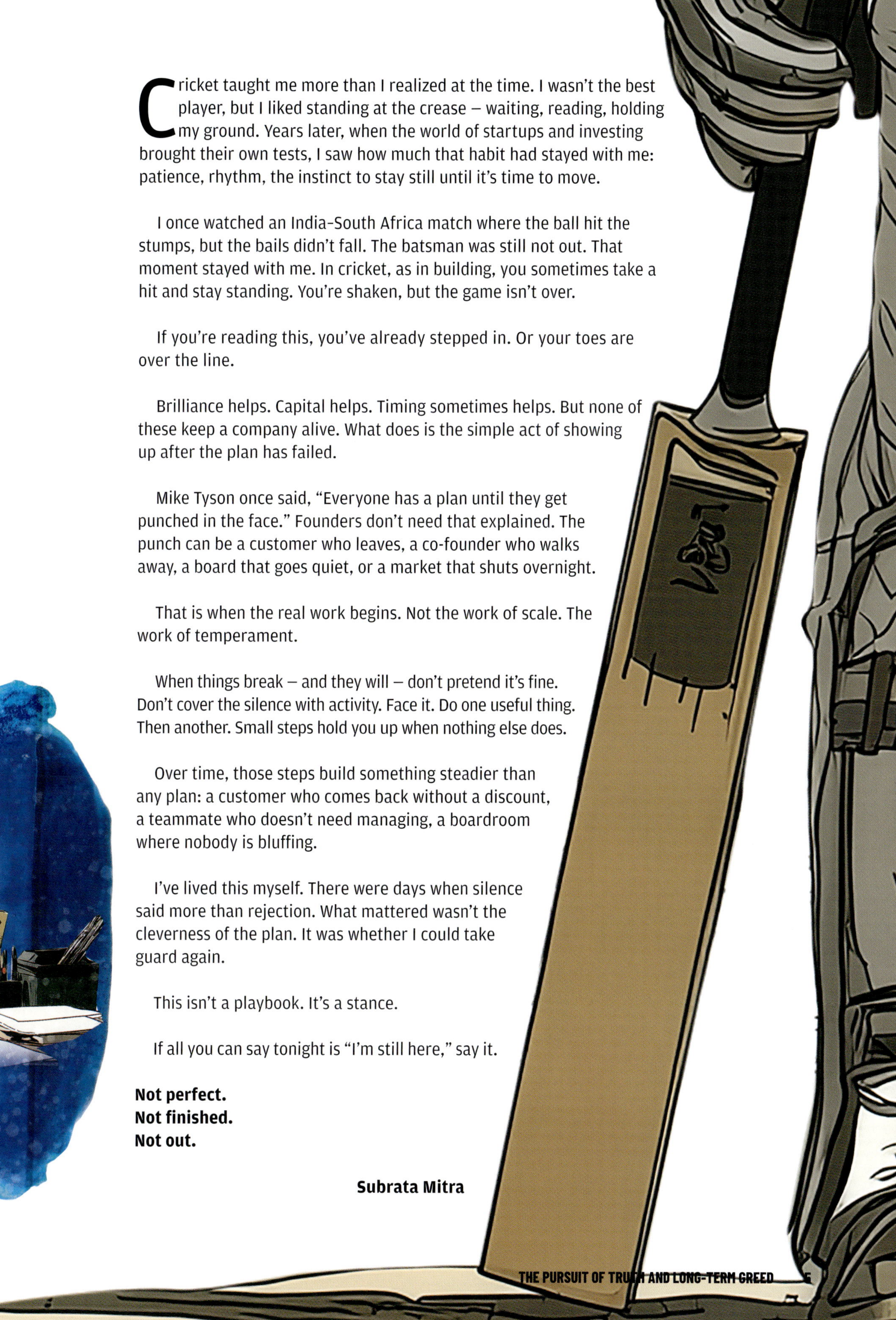

Cricket taught me more than I realized at the time. I wasn't the best player, but I liked standing at the crease – waiting, reading, holding my ground. Years later, when the world of startups and investing brought their own tests, I saw how much that habit had stayed with me: patience, rhythm, the instinct to stay still until it's time to move.

I once watched an India-South Africa match where the ball hit the stumps, but the bails didn't fall. The batsman was still not out. That moment stayed with me. In cricket, as in building, you sometimes take a hit and stay standing. You're shaken, but the game isn't over.

If you're reading this, you've already stepped in. Or your toes are over the line.

Brilliance helps. Capital helps. Timing sometimes helps. But none of these keep a company alive. What does is the simple act of showing up after the plan has failed.

Mike Tyson once said, "Everyone has a plan until they get punched in the face." Founders don't need that explained. The punch can be a customer who leaves, a co-founder who walks away, a board that goes quiet, or a market that shuts overnight.

That is when the real work begins. Not the work of scale. The work of temperament.

When things break – and they will – don't pretend it's fine. Don't cover the silence with activity. Face it. Do one useful thing. Then another. Small steps hold you up when nothing else does.

Over time, those steps build something steadier than any plan: a customer who comes back without a discount, a teammate who doesn't need managing, a boardroom where nobody is bluffing.

I've lived this myself. There were days when silence said more than rejection. What mattered wasn't the cleverness of the plan. It was whether I could take guard again.

This isn't a playbook. It's a stance.

If all you can say tonight is "I'm still here," say it.

Not perfect.
Not finished.
Not out.

Subrata Mitra

Entrepreneurship isn't about avoiding close calls; it's surviving them. Like a batsman at the crease, bails barely holding – still standing, still uncertain, yet still in the game. Not perfect, not done, but not out.

My father once nudged my head away from a mithai-shop window without a word. I didn't know he had lost his job; I only felt the quiet weight of his hand guiding me forward.

A few months later I recorded myself saying, "When my father finds his job, I'll tie it down so it can never run away."
When he finally did, two cars stood in our driveway – a white Ambassador (WBC 7350) and a blue Standard Herald (WBJ 894). For me, they were proof that life had steadied again.

LEARNING TO READ THE SIGNS

I've often been asked where it began – this way of reading people, companies, markets. I think it started in Kolkata, long before I knew what resilience meant.

At four years old, you don't know the word for loss, but you feel it. It shows up in gestures – small enough to be invisible to everyone else, unforgettable to you.

It was the late sixties, an evening on a Kolkata street – oil crackling in jalebi pans, smoke lifting from charcoal, the clang of cycle bells threading through the noise. My father had taken me along for errands, his hand firm around mine.

We passed the mithai shop, its glass case glowing under low bulbs: sandesh stacked in precise rows, rosogollas swaying in syrup. Without thinking, my head tilted toward the window.

And then I felt it – his hand on the back of my head, steady but not rough, guiding my gaze forward. No words, no reprimand. Just a deliberate correction. I didn't know then that he'd lost his job. I couldn't see the strain he kept from my mother, my sister, and me. But I felt it in that quiet gesture.

Months later, another moment stayed with me. I was at a neighbor's house, in a plain, sunlit room. On the table sat my most prized possession – a plastic tape recorder, bright-colored, its oversized buttons worn from use. I pressed record, leaned in, and said: "When my father finds his job, I will tie it down so tight, it can never run away."

My neighbor was startled. She came across to our home and played it aloud. My father sat behind me, newspaper open, shoulders slightly bent. He didn't turn. He didn't comment. But I know he heard it. That was enough.

Stability returned later, without announcement. One evening I stood in our driveway and saw two cars parked neatly side by side again. Behind the curtains, the light was warm, the air steady. Nothing was said. Life had simply found its balance again.

My father never spoke about resilience. He showed it – in the way he carried setbacks without spilling them into the room, in how he kept the family's head pointed forward. Years later, in my own collapses – empty offices, companies shutting down in silence – I went back to those images: the hand at the back of my head, the promise whispered into a recorder, the sight of two cars in the driveway. Quiet proofs that loss can be carried, and that life rights itself.

Lessons like that don't arrive as revelations. They're stored in gestures and silences. And you only understand them years later – when you need them most.

Don Bosco School, Kolkata. Young Subrata Mitra long before "learning to read the signs" became his way of navigating the world.

NOT JUST ANOTHER DEGREE

I entered IIT Kanpur in 1984 with a full head of hair I refused to comb. Literal, yes – but mostly habit. From day one, I had a system. I'd attend the first class of every course, quietly evaluate the professor, and if they didn't meet my internal bar, I stopped showing up. I kept learning anyway.

My real education happened in the hostel corridors – at midnight, knocking on doors, whispering: "*Tu bina notes diye kaise so gaya?*" I studied off Dinesh's perfect notes, decoded Arup's meticulous transcripts, and needled Sudeep's consistency with quick checks of my own. We weren't just classmates; we were each other's parallel curriculum.

Linear Algebra became my case study in nonconformity. I skipped every lecture and showed up only for the fourteen quizzes. After three straight zeros, I sat beside Sudeep Sarkar for the fourth. Halfway through, I noticed he was dividing by a zero determinant. "Boss, I don't know the right answer, but yours is definitely wrong," I whispered. We both scored zero. His respect didn't drop. Mine rose for him too. We still laugh about it.

By third year, the GRE fever had overtaken campus. I'd barely heard of it. That summer, I went home, spoke with my parents, and decided to try. My score was unremarkable. The top twenty schools passed. But a professor at the University of Delaware – an IIT Kanpur alum – looked at my file and offered a fellowship. That yes changed everything.

Delaware was my first experience outside India. A snow-covered campus. Microwaves. First-name introductions. No Dinesh or Sudeep to lean on. Just me. Class attendance became survival. I adapted – graduated with a 4.0, straight A's – and realized I could hold my own anywhere.

From there, I moved to the University of Illinois for a PhD under Nachum Dershowitz – a brilliant, unstructured, deeply trusting advisor. His line stayed with me: "Don't try to be clever. Try to be precise." That sentence has quietly shaped everything since.

Two moments from those years never left me.

One was a talk by a visiting alum – a founder of a financial software company. Someone asked how he'd made a fortune doing what he was good at. He turned to the whiteboard and wrote "$90 million," and stopped. This is what he made after selling his company. He titled his talk "How to make a fortune doing what you love."

The other was in my own classroom. A tall, tired classmate who often borrowed my notes turned out to be one of Netscape's co-founders (Chris Houck). Back then, he wasn't a legend – just someone who coded all night and slept through lectures. Years later, when I learned who he was, it made the idea of building suddenly tangible. This wasn't a myth. It was happening down the hallway.

By 1994, I was married, had two cars, about twenty thousand dollars saved, and had paid for my wife's master's. I defended my PhD and joined IBM. Ashish Gupta was in the database group; I was in applications. We'd meet for coffee. Then he moved to Oracle and soon co-founded Junglee. Watching him build, scale, and sell wasn't envy – it was ignition. If he could walk through that door, maybe I could too.

That's how ECT happened. Bhaskar, an old Andersen Consulting colleague, and I tried to build a product to ease the pain of ERP implementations. Four people. Vague idea. No shipped product. It was ego theatre. The company faded before it formed.

Firewhite came later. We raised real capital. Hired people who left safer jobs to bet on us. Built serious tech. Signed early customers. After 9/11, budgets froze. We slipped into irrelevance. That reckoning belongs elsewhere in this chapter. Here, it's enough to say it changed me – and forced clearer choices.

One choice was personal. I'd met Sagarika through a matrimonial ad my father had placed in 1991. We married in December 1992, and moved to the University of Illinois Urbana-Champaign where Sagarika joined the MS program.

She was clear from the beginning: we would return to India. I thought she would change her mind once she saw the U.S. I had a U.S. Green Card, friends, and momentum in the Valley, but the decision was black and white. We came back on January 8, 1998.

I didn't think of it as a "second innings." I thought of it as removing the gray. From that point on, the choices that mattered would be decisive, not deferred.

Degrees look good on a résumé. But when they stop helping, and trust is placed in you, the real learning starts – not in classrooms, but in choices. Life has its grayscale. When the moment comes, your decision must be black and white.

Subrata and Sagarika met in 1991 through a matrimonial ad his father had placed. Before marriage, she made her condition clear: they would not settle in the U.S. "I'll marry you, but you have to return to India in three or four years." They did – moving back for good in 1998.

THE HARD WAY

When I meet founders now, I ask:

"Have your customers hurt your feelings yet?"

Because until you've faced that polite indifference – the smile that hides we don't need you – you haven't started your real education.

Girish Mathrubootham once told me, "I dream in installments." Not billion-dollar leaps. Just ten million, then fifty, then a hundred – each milestone anchored in what customers were actually feeling, not what the slides claimed. That discipline is the difference between proximity to truth and the illusion of traction.

I learned this the hard way.

My first startup, ECT, came through Bhaskar – an old Andersen Consulting colleague. India in the late '90s made product companies work hard; we felt that pull. We were swimming against gravity, but in truth, we never even went deep enough to feel the full drag. There were no layoffs, no cash burn, no customers to disappoint. Four of us sat around a table, clever at debate, shallow in execution. The egos lasted longer than the company. When it ended, it didn't hurt. It just ended.

Firewhite was different.

This time, we raised real capital. Hired serious people – many of whom left stable jobs to join us. Built technology that worked and signed early customers. On paper it looked right: résumés from Apple and IBM, investors nodding, a pitch about enterprises moving from laptops to early smartphones – BlackBerry, Palm OS, pocket PCs – devices we believed were inevitable. Our solution – remote management and security – felt obvious.

But we were never essential. Our customers took meetings, smiled, and nodded. Not one ever said, "If you shut down tomorrow, it will hurt us." One investor put it plainly: "You talk to all these customers, but none has said they'll hurt if you disappear tomorrow." That line landed like a verdict. At the end of it, I became good friends with this investor.

When the market turned after 9/11, there was no dramatic crash – there was attrition. Meetings got harder to book, pilots slowed, the distance between our product and urgent customer pain widened until it felt obvious. Erosion, not explosion.

We had exactly four customers. When I sent our shutdown email, only one replied – an apologetic call and a small acquisition offer, due to a combination of need and compassion. The other three never answered. Their silence cut deeper than rejection. I learned then the cruelest business signal isn't a no. It's indifference.

With ECT, failure felt diffuse – an unfinished rehearsal. With Firewhite, there was no one else to blame. It wasn't the market. It wasn't the team. It wasn't the idea. It was my judgment. I sat across people who had bet years of their lives on me and told them it was over – not theatrically, but finally.

For weeks I couldn't sleep. Couldn't eat. I replayed every customer meeting, every polite nod I'd mistaken for permission. Accountability stopped being an abstract line item; it lodged in my body – tight in my chest, hollow in my stomach, lead in my limbs.

On those nights I remembered a documentary I'd half-watched years earlier: a desert mouse stung by a scorpion, stunned, then slowly stirring. Nature had equipped it with an anti-venom – a silent, physiological resilience that let it outlast the scorpion.

Entrepreneurship is like that. Failure stuns you. But somewhere inside there is an anti-venom – a private, painful muscle called accountability – that, slowly, lets you stand up again.

In India we have another image: Shiva, the Neelkanth, who swallowed poison meant for the world. The poison left a mark on him, but he lived. Founders carry similar marks. The poison is responsibility – for people, for promises, for decisions no one else will own.

Years later I saw the same posture in other founders like Sachin and Binny of Flipkart. That fateful Big Billion Day when our systems failed miserably and Sachin's open letter...is truly a mark of a legendary company being born.

People ask me where I was truly shaped – was it IIT, Illinois, IBM, the Valley? I tell them no. My real schooling happened in the silence after Firewhite – when there was nowhere left to look but inward, when the only question left was: Do I still belong here, in the world of entrepreneurship?

I didn't answer with words. I answered by showing up again. Repeatedly. Quietly. Without applause.

That taught me the only principle I trust:

Life is mostly grayscale – polite nods, ambiguous signals – but when the moment comes, your decision must be black and white.

You swallow the poison.
You keep moving.
It's bitter medicine.

But it heals.

EGO ON THE TABLE

After returning from the Valley, I teamed up with my Andersen colleague, Bhaskar. We had the ideas and the drive—but not the customer. It ended before it began.

It was a superficial failure. A few people sitting around a table thinking we'll build something. Ego got the better of all of us.

THE BUBBLE OF ISOLATION

The company didn't implode—it quietly emptied out. No dramatic exit, no press release. Just a final email. The hardest part wasn't letting go. It was admitting it was already over.

I could not eat. I could not sleep. The weight of my responsibility toward my employees and investors was crushing.

MAPPING IN FOG

Startups don't begin with certainty. They begin in the fog.

I've told founders this more than once – half in jest, fully in truth: "I can probably see slightly better than you, hopefully. But it's still foggy and misty." That's the job. No matter how many times you've built, you're still squinting into partial light. The map is never anywhere close to being complete. It shifts under your feet. But still, you must draw more.

Early-stage leadership is not about conviction in a destination. It's about walking into uncertainty with enough steadiness that others will follow. You don't promise clarity. You promise presence. You absorb ambiguity without freezing. You hold the line not because the path is clear, but because you've decided to keep moving anyway.

That's where my own metaphor emerged: truth is the map, long-term greed is the compass.

The map isn't a quarterly dashboard. It's what you unfold every morning. It shows you where you really are: the customer's silence, the trust that's eroding, the feature that broke something you didn't notice. The map is rarely flattering. Sometimes it tells you you're further behind than you'd like to admit.

The compass isn't a plan. It's orientation. It points you to what will last ten years from now, not what looks good this quarter. A customer who comes back without a discount. A teammate who doesn't need managing. A boardroom where nobody is bluffing.

In India, the fog is thicker. The maps are less detailed. You won't always have data or benchmarks. But you can still choose a direction, and you can redraw as the terrain changes. That is the work.

When we started Erasmic, there was no strategy deck, no thesis. We didn't start with power. We started with doubt. Trust – earned slowly, by showing up – was our only real asset. And in the fog, that was enough.

The terrain keeps changing. The fog never clears completely. But if you keep your map close, your compass steady, and your pencil moving, you'll find your way through.

HOW ERASMIC WAS REALLY BUILT

We didn't begin with a fund or a thesis. What we had were questions. Why was it so hard for Indian entrepreneurs to find someone who believed in them before the slide decks? Why did capital always seem to arrive with distance built in?

It was 2004. Firewhite had collapsed, and I was grinding through operations at Tavant. I wasn't looking to raise money. I wanted to work with founders again, but this time closer, earlier – but I didn't want to be the one holding it all together this time.

Later in the year, one evening I met my batchmate Gagan Kumar at the Koramangala Club in Bangalore. We weren't talking about strategy. We were talking about what we wished we'd had when we were starting up. Sitting on plastic chairs, lukewarm tea between us, we asked: what would it mean to sit across from a founder and say, I'm with you – before anyone else did?

At a nearby table, Mahendran Balachandran had just wrapped up a meeting. He had returned from Apple not long before, quietly easing into his next chapter. He caught pieces of our conversation.

Later, he asked Gagan, "Who was your friend? What are you two building?" The next day Gagan called me. "Even if I don't join you, there's someone who might." Soon, Mahendran was at the table. He listened more than he spoke. At the end he said, without ceremony, "If you need another partner, I'm in." No more than that. No pitch, no paperwork. Just presence.

The fourth seat was Prashanth Prakash. I had first met him at Delaware in graduate school, then lost touch. Years later, when I was still at Tavant, I walked into NetKraft's office in Bangalore looking for a desk. In the corner, behind a computer, Prashanth looked up. "Subrata?" That was all. We didn't need to explain. The connection was still there. We said we would do something entrepreneurial together soon, and it was still early 2004.

That is how Erasmic began. The three of us without any roles, or a strategy deck. Just a promise: let's write the kind of checks we wished we had received. We called it Erasmic, after Erasmus, the Renaissance thinker who built bridges across languages and worlds. It wasn't branding; it was instinct. We didn't yet have the words for what we were trying to build.

Fundraising was unglamorous. I flew economy to the U.S., stayed in budget motels, and called people who had worked with me at IBM or Illinois, or who had backed me before. No cold emails. No pitch documents. Just: "You've seen what I've tried to build. Will you trust me again?" Many said no. Ashish Gupta, who had been my colleague at IBM and had gone on to co-found Junglee, kept repeating to others, "Subrata has built before. He will build again." His vouch counted more than any credential of mine.

Our first check went to Mu Sigma. We used to call it "Fund Zero." It wasn't based on a market map. It was based on the founder. Later came Scripbox. I had seen Betterment in Palo Alto and called Atul Shinghal in India: "Can we do this here?" Then Ninjacart, Moglix, Mensa. None came through a pipeline. They came through conversations, through being available when the idea changed, through instinct followed by follow-through.

Each of us brought something different. Mahendran slowed us down, but always got the details right. Gagan carried founder empathy. Prashanth kept the tempo. My instinct was always to go first. At Delaware, on the cricket field, when no one wanted to open, I'd say, "Give me the bat." Not to impress, but because hesitation has to be broken by action. That habit never left me. If a founder was uncertain, my default was to say, "I'll go first. Follow me."

Over time, I realized what made Erasmic work wasn't just the people. It was the posture. Early-stage investing is like drawing maps in fog. You can only see a little further than the rest: a ridge, a break in the trees, a faint outline through mist. The fog never clears completely.

In that fog, you need two tools: a map and a compass. The map is the truth – the lived reality you unfold every day. Not the version on a pitch deck, but the customer's silence, the feature that broke something else, the trust that is fraying. The compass is long-term greed. Not a rigid plan, but an orientation: choosing what will matter in ten years over what looks good in a quarterly update. That's what keeps you from drifting when the terrain shifts.

We didn't start Erasmic with power. We started with doubt. The only thing we had was trust, earned slowly by showing up. The fog has never lifted completely. But with the map close, the compass steady, and the discipline to keep drawing as we go, we've always found a way forward.

UNSEEN COSTS

I often think of the Neelkanth story – of Shiva swallowing poison to protect others. He survived, but it scarred him forever. Founders aren't gods, and this isn't mythology. But there is a parallel: you often absorb the stress so others don't have to. You carry the weight quietly. The team may never notice. But your family always does.

For years, I told myself I could keep those worlds separate – carry the poison outside and leave it at the door. It doesn't work that way. Detachment isn't a decision; it's a slow drift. You come home physically, but not fully. You're at the dinner table, but your mind is still turning over a churned customer, a term sheet, or the meeting you know will be hard tomorrow. You become quieter without meaning to, and the people closest to you notice before you do. Once, my son said, "You're always busy, even when you're here." That one stayed with me.

The costs aren't just at home. They show up in friendships – especially when you start a company with people you've known for years. Friendship is unconditional. Co-founding is full of conditions: performance, priorities, pain thresholds. When those diverge, the fracture isn't just operational; it's personal. You don't just lose a partner. You lose the weddings, the festivals, the easy shorthand you thought was permanent. Some of those friendships didn't survive my early companies.

And then there's the hardest cost of all – letting people go. In the Valley, it's procedural. In India, it's personal. You're not just firing an employee. You're sitting across from the person who played cricket with you on Sundays, who brought food when your mom was in the hospital, or even donated blood for another employee. You tell them, "This role no longer exists," and the look in their eyes doesn't say, "I lost a job." It says, "You let me down."

In those moments, you're forced to confront something no business book prepares you for: the reflection staring back at you. You can rationalize the decision. You can point to the numbers. But alone, you have to ask the harder question – did I fail them? That's the mirror test. After every one of those conversations, I've gone home and sat with that question longer than with any metric or milestone.

I thought of that when Raghu left TaxiForSure. From the outside, it looked like a standard founder exit. But when he called, it wasn't about the transaction. It was about the disorientation of watching something you'd built become someone else's. We hung up, and I just sat there – no consolations, no philosophy. Just recognition. I knew the terrain. I'd walked it before.

These costs don't appear on a P&L. They collect quietly – in the way your family learns to read your silences, in the empathy you feel when another founder's chapter closes. Over time, you get better at carrying them. You don't shed them. You mark them. Not as scars to display, not as warnings. Just proof that you were the one who swallowed what no one else wanted to.

- Family
- Friendships
- Time away from my son when he was growing up
- US trips that were for 2 days & 2 meetings
- Torn between shareholder responsibilites & founders' ambition!

GANNA JUICE – ONE MORE TURN

I still remember an evening near IIT Kanpur's Hall 1, long after the summer sun had slipped low. The air carried the layered sounds of campus life – students drifting back from labs, the clang of bicycle stands, bursts of laughter from hostel corridors.

At the edge of the bazaar, I stopped at a sugarcane juice stall. The vendor, in a faded kurta, worked an old iron press – two heavy rollers groaning with each turn of the flywheel. The first pass was easy: pale-green juice poured quickly into a steel jug, with cubes of ice already in it.

What struck me was what came next. The crushed stalks, fibrous and seemingly dry, were tossed onto a growing pile. But then the vendor picked them up again. He shifted their angle, twisted them slightly, sprinkled some water over them, and fed them back through the rollers. The rollers needed a lot more pressure this time. A thin trickle emerged. Not as sweet, not as much – but still juice. Still something left.

That image has stayed with me. Because building in India rarely happens in one clean sweep. It is not one launch, one success, one straight line upward. It is the repeated turning of the stalk – coming back to something that looks finished, changing your grip, and discovering it still has more to give. And the ice water could be a bridge round or even a new CXO.

The discipline is the same: persistence in small, unglamorous turns. Adjusting quietly when the first effort falls short. Revisiting a problem that looked exhausted. Returning to work with patience. From those turns, momentum comes back.

The sugarcane vendor wasn't in a hurry, and he wasn't frustrated. He worked steadily, as if he knew each twist still mattered. On the hardest days in my own journey – when ECT ended before it really began, when Firewhite faded into silence – I've thought of that calm. The habit of picking up the stalk one more time, adjusting the grip and trying again.

When I sit across from a tired founder today, I don't offer speeches. I just say: "Maybe, we need to try one more turn."

And almost always, something emerges. Not a flood. Not a miracle. But enough. Enough to keep going.

TEMPERED LIKE GOLD

The inspiring story of India's telecom product aspirations and the making of a product nation

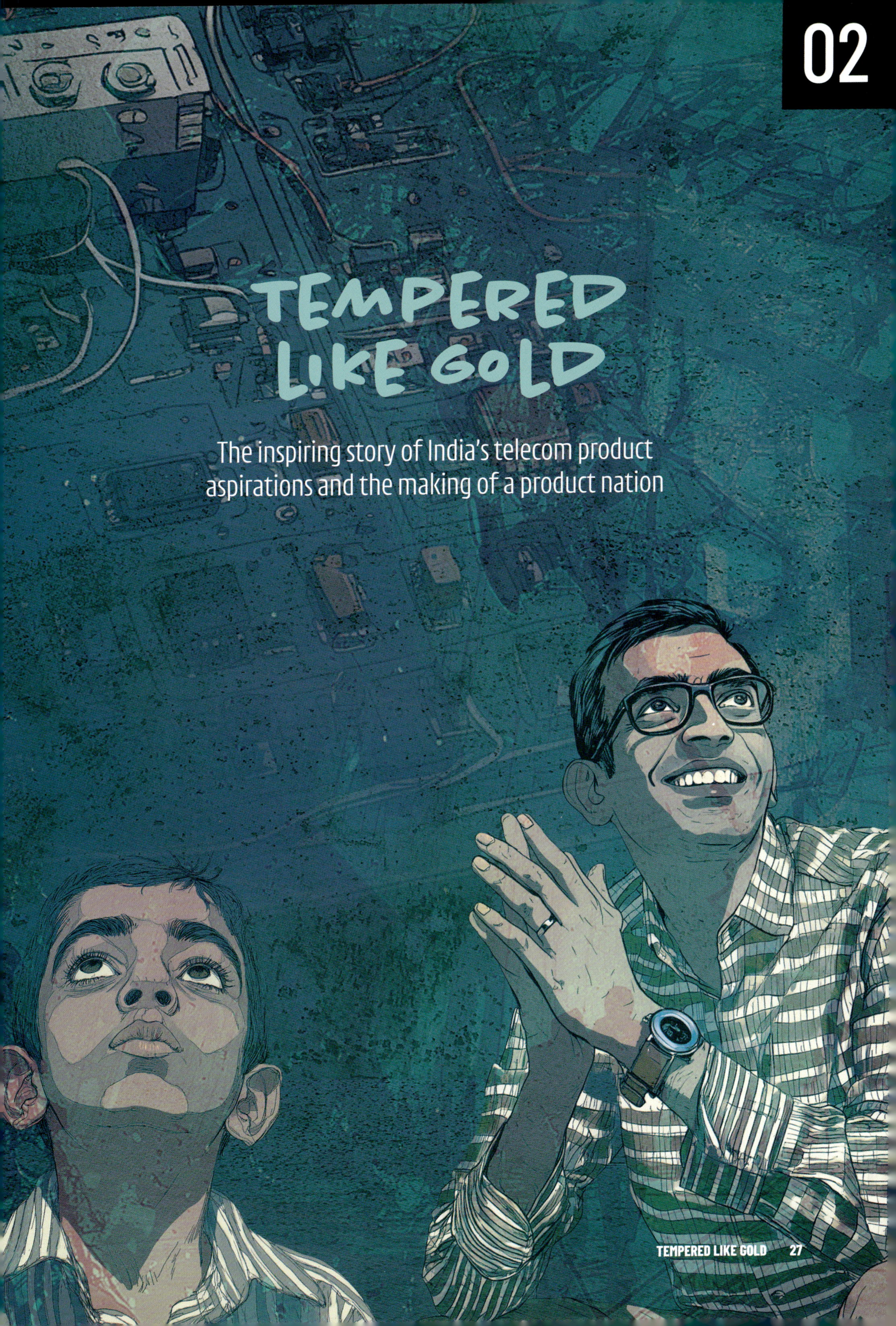

Fire in Bangalore Labs

This is not only the story of Sanjay Nayak.

It is the story of Tejas Networks – of his co-founders Arnob Roy, Kumar N. Sivarajan, their mentor Gururaj Desh Deshpande, and of the hundreds of others: engineers who kept R&D labs running through uncertainty, salespeople who won customer confidence, factory operators who held the assembly lines steady during floods, investors who stayed patient for decades, and customers who chose an untested Indian company when global giants offered safer options.

It is the story of a company, and a country slowly learning to believe in its ability to design and build world-class products. It is the story of India's telecom product aspirations, and a lesson in what it will take for India to become a product nation.

Over two decades, from 2000 to 2025, Tejas faced financial shocks, market freezes, floods, and even fire. To understand the calm resolve, Sanjay showed as flames gutted his office, you have to first understand these lives – the collective endurance, and the long years of steady, unglamorous effort that made survival possible in moments of crisis.

In 2012, a fire tore through Tejas's Bangalore R&D labs, erasing years of work in hours and leaving its founders to decide whether the company itself could be rebuilt.

FROM MADHYA PRADESH TO BOSTON

Sanjay Nayak's childhood unfolded in towns that existed only because a dam was being built nearby. His father, a civil engineer with the Madhya Pradesh government, moved from one project site to the next – remote postings with erratic electricity, rough roads, and little infrastructure. Home was never a fixed address; it was wherever concrete and steel were being poured into a rising wall.

At ten, Sanjay was sent to Rajkumar College in Raipur, a boarding school chosen to give him stability. He arrived with a suitcase and no script. The school was not harsh, but it did not cushion him either. Independence was assumed, and he had to learn it quickly. That early training in self-reliance left a deeper mark than any lecture could have.

During breaks, he returned to the dam sites. He saw his father shoulder responsibility without complaint – problems solved one by one, deadlines met in harsh conditions, dignity intact. Years later, when floods submerged Tejas's Pondicherry factory or fire gutted its Bangalore R&D labs, Sanjay would recognize the same lesson: don't panic, don't posture, just keep working until the way forward appears.

He landed at BIT Mesra almost by accident – missing the IIT entrance exam by an hour. The campus on the outskirts of Ranchi offered basic labs and a single computer center that was always crowded. Electronics and Communications was the practical choice. There he built a rhythm: understand an efficient way to crack exams, and still leave time for sports and campus life. That efficiency gave him confidence that adaptation itself was a skill.

A scholarship took him to North Carolina State University. The scale of the labs and the pace of research were overwhelming at first, but the method held. He rose to the top of his classes, and years later the university placed him in its Hall of Fame, recognizing both his academic work and his career in technology.

After his graduation, he joined Gateway Design Automation, a thirty-person startup in Boston, Massachusetts. Gateway had invented the Verilog hardware description language, which fundamentally transformed how chip and electronics would be designed. For Sanjay, it was apprenticeship in the truest sense: working alongside pioneers, building tools that shaped an entire industry, and seeing what it took to make technology at the frontier. When Cadence acquired Gateway in 1989 and set up an R&D center in Noida, the decision to return to India was clear. It was an opportunity to help build world-class products at home – long before such moves were fashionable.

The path from dam sites in Madhya Pradesh to labs in Boston was anything but straight. But through each turn, the habits carried through: adapt quickly, persist through difficulty, and work with dignity under pressure. Those became the deeper roots of everything Tejas would one day stand on.

From dam sites with no fixed home to a Raipur boarding school at ten, Sanjay's early years were shaped by transience and self-reliance.

TAKING THE ENTERPRENEURSHIP PLUNGE

By the late 1990s, Sanjay had built a comfortable career. At Synopsys, one of the world's leading electronic design automation firms, he was climbing steadily. The work was global, the pay secure, and the arc predictable. For many, it would have been the summit.

But comfort became a dilemma. At every strategy review, the same refrain echoed: the United States decided, India executed. The pattern was clear – the country was becoming indispensable to the global technology industry, but as a supplier of talent and services, not as a creator of products.

It was during this period that Sanjay connected with Deshpande, one of the earliest Indians to build a billion-dollar tech company in the United States. Deshpande had shown that Indian engineers could not only execute but also conceive and scale frontier products. His advice was blunt: if India was to prove itself, someone had to stop climbing the MNC corporate ladder and start building a product company at home.

The decision was not simple. Synopsys offered certainty. Entrepreneurship in India offered risk, against an ecosystem that hardly existed. But the imbalance gnawed: to stay meant accepting the comfort of execution without authorship; to leave meant testing whether an Indian company could design and manufacture complex telecom products for the world.

In 2000, Sanjay chose to leave. With Arnob and Kumar, and with Deshpande's backing, he founded Tejas Networks. It was less a career move than a wager: that India could no longer remain content being the back office of the world, and that its engineers could – if given the chance – build products at the same standard as their peers in Boston, Silicon Valley, or anywhere else.

STAY
USA
→ Recognition
→ Safety
→ Dollars
GO
INDIA
→ uncertainty
→ Struggle
→ Obscurity

SEEDING AN ECOSYSTEM

When Tejas Networks was founded in 2000, the idea that India could design and manufacture its own telecom equipment to global standards was close to unthinkable. The country had IT services firms scaling rapidly, but there was no ecosystem for deep-tech product companies.

If Tejas was to survive, it had to help create the very conditions it needed. That meant building not just products, but the scaffolding around them: policy frameworks that would give domestic products a fair chance in government bids, investors willing to stay patient through long gestation cycles, and manufacturing partners who could help deliver products that offered five-nines reliability – 99.999% uptime – without precedent. It also meant persuading bright engineers to leave stable MNC jobs, and convincing early customers that choosing an Indian-designed product was not charity but foresight.

The risks were obvious. At the time, nearly every piece of telecom hardware in India came fully built from abroad. Manufacturing locally was considered reckless – one flaw could take down an entire network. Customers choosing India-designed products was even more far-fetched. But Sanjay and his co-founders decided Tejas would stay focused on high-leverage R&D and sales, while entrusting manufacturing to specialists.

In 2001, Flextronics opened one of India's first serious Electronics Manufacturing Services (EMS) facilities in Bangalore's Electronic City. Tejas became its anchor customer. Handing over production to a new team raised doubts among customers, partners, even some of Tejas's own engineers. To make it work, Tejas engineers worked side by side with Flextronics staff – guiding processes, supervising quality checks, and fixing sourcing problems in real time. Every unit that left the line was tested exhaustively. Slowly, confidence replaced skepticism.

As Tejas products passed the same global benchmarks as equipment from Singapore or China, other EMS majors – Sanmina, Jabil, Celestica – followed Flextronics into India. What began as a necessity for one company became the seed of an industry.

Each of these steps – policy advocacy, investor persuasion, talent recruitment, customer trust, and outsourcing to EMS – was a brick in the product ecosystem. Without them, there would have been no foundation for Tejas, and no platform on which India's deep-tech ambitions could stand.

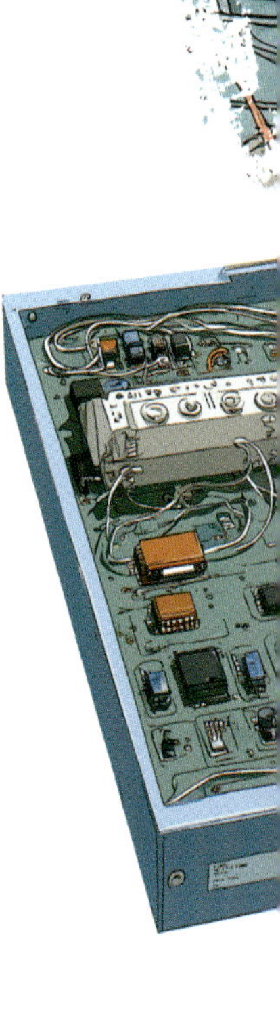

A Decade of Wins

WHEN THE CLIMB PEAKED

By 2009, Tejas Networks looked unstoppable. Revenues had climbed from ₹5 crore in its first year to ₹676 crore in nine years. The team had grown to seven hundred. Five rounds of funding had brought in $100 million from blue-chip investors. Products designed in Bangalore were being shipped to more than fifty countries. Nortel, a global giant, sold Tejas gear under its own label. Awards came from the prime minister's office and Harvard Business School wrote a case study.

Inside the company, the momentum felt inevitable. Plans were drawn to take Tejas public. The Goldman Sachs pre-IPO round in 2008 seemed the last step before listing. For a brief moment, it appeared that India had created a deep-tech company that could not only match the world but also lead it.

But beneath the numbers, fragility was already showing. Tejas depended heavily on Nortel for exports. The domestic telecom market was beginning to wobble. In the background, storms were gathering that would soon undo much of what had been built.

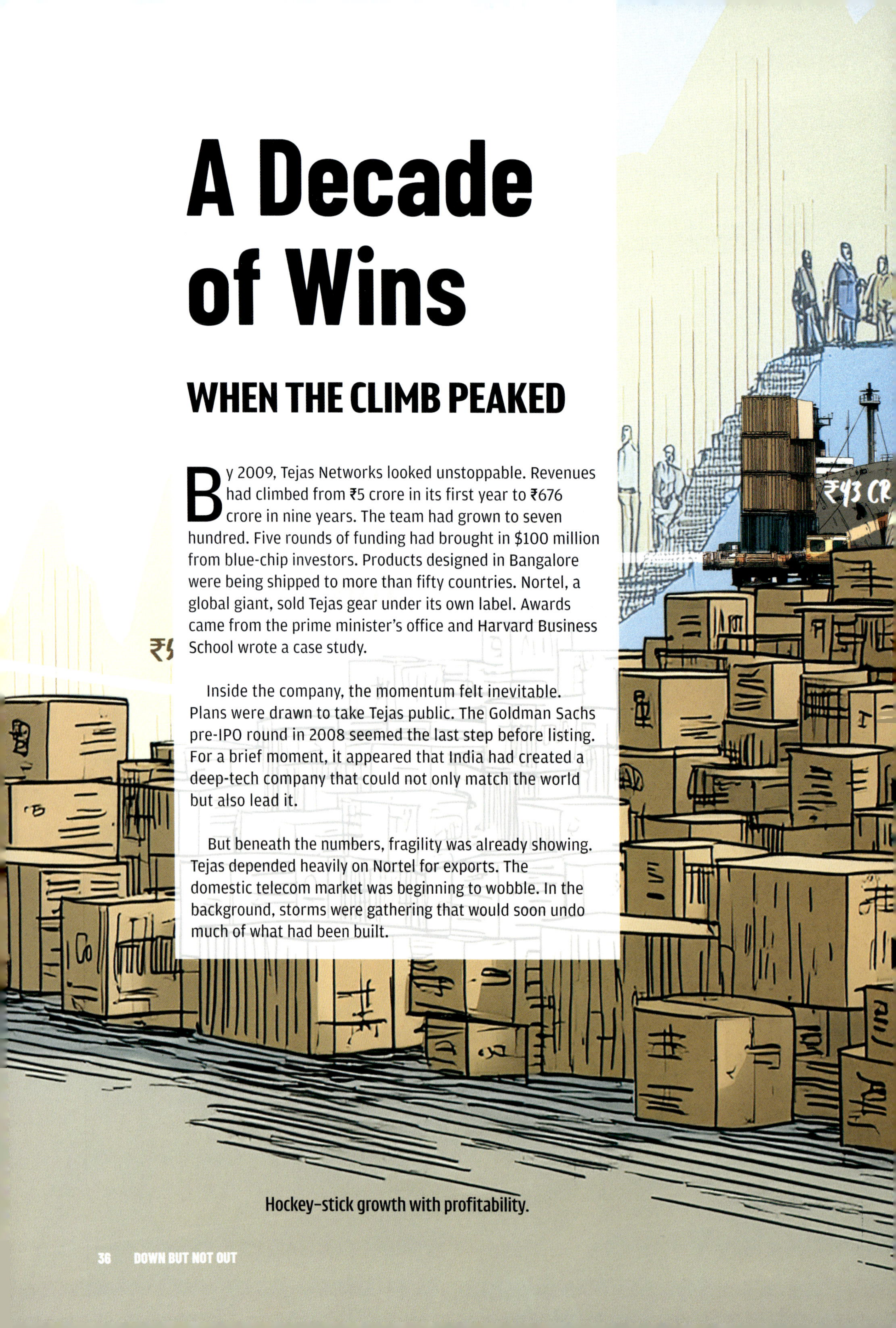

Hockey-stick growth with profitability.

$100mn
₹676 CR
₹350 CR
₹223 CR
₹115CR

THE WALL STREET JOURNA
AIG, Lehman Shock Hits World Mar
NORTEL

Crisis Stack

WHAT SURVIVED THE FIRE

Then the blows landed in sequence. Lehman's collapse froze the IPO window. Nortel declared bankruptcy, wiping out Tejas's largest export customer. The 2G scam brought Indian telecom capex to a standstill. Cyclone Thane flooded the Pondicherry plant in 2011. A year later, fire gutted the Bangalore R&D labs.

Revenues fell from ₹676 crore in 2009 to ₹208 crore by 2012. Cost-cutting was necessary and doing layoffs seemed inevitable; even managers expected cuts. But Sanjay, Arnob, and Kumar refused. For them, Tejas's survival rested on capability, not headcount.

Instead, senior leaders took pay cuts. Salaries were delayed, raises frozen, bonuses postponed. Even in the trough year, with revenues of just ₹208 crore, Tejas invested close to a third of turnover into R&D. It was a gamble: if new products were not ready when the market turned, there would be nothing left to save.

Employees stayed. Some because they believed in the mission, others because they trusted the founders and wanted to prove that an Indian company could build world-class products through the worst. Out of that stubbornness came the one thing the fire could not erase: a culture of persistence that carried Tejas into its next chapter.

Between 2008 and 2013, Tejas lost customers, revenue, and labs – but not its key people.

After losses, floods, fire, and near collapse, Tejas bet on R&D, rebuilt its platforms, and returned to the markets with India's first deep-tech IPO.

THE LONG ROAD BACK TO THE BELL

By 2012, Tejas Networks was running on thin air. Revenues had dropped to ₹208 crore, losses mounted, and the sequence of blows – global financial crisis, Nortel's bankruptcy, the 2G scam, floods, and fire – had left the company battered. Conventional logic said survival demanded layoffs. Salaries were the largest cost, and cutting staff would buy instant breathing room.

The founders took the harder route. They chose to hold the team together, betting that capability, not cost-cutting, was the only chance of recovery. Every rupee that could be spared went into R&D.

In that trough year, with revenues of just ₹208 crore, Tejas still invested close to a third of its turnover in product development. It was a wager many would call reckless, but Sanjay and his co-founders were convinced that unless they were ready with next-generation platforms when the market turned, there would be no company left to save.

Inside the labs, engineers worked on a platform reboot – moving from voice-era products to data-era architectures. The sales team, forced to survive without a single dominant customer, pushed to diversify. Each small contract became proof the company was still alive.

The climb back was slow but unmistakable: from ₹208 crore in 2012 to ₹275 → ₹394 → ₹625 → ₹865 crore by 2017. Profitability returned. Tejas stood again at the threshold of the public markets.

When the IPO bell rang in 2017, it was hailed as India's first pure deep-tech product IPO. For those inside, the listing was less about the capital raised than the validation it carried.

The market was not just rewarding a balance sheet. It was recognizing a strong commitment to the mission of building world-class products from India, seventeen years of resilience across business cycles, a culture that refused to give up on its people, and a product line rebuilt brick by brick.

WHEN THE MARKET TURNED, TEJAS WAS READY

For two decades, Tejas Networks had been proving something India wasn't ready to believe – that its own engineers could design and build complex telecom equipment at world-class standards. The technology was never the problem; from the early years Tejas products matched international benchmarks. The barrier was belief. Procurement policies required proof of large global deployments before awarding major Indian contracts, a catch-22 that kept homegrown firms locked out. Operators saw foreign brands as the safe choice. India's most critical networks were being built with imported hardware, often financed by foreign credit lines.

That equilibrium broke in mid-2020. A violent clash at Galwan Valley brought the risks of dependence on Chinese suppliers into sharp focus. Suddenly, procurement policy shifted. What had once been dismissed as Tejas's private lament – that India must trust its own products – became national priority under the banner of strategic autonomy.

The first test came quickly. BSNL was tasked with executing a nationwide 4G rollout built entirely on indigenous technology. It meant 100,000 base stations, one of the largest deployments in the world, to be delivered in just eighteen months. Tejas had been preparing for this moment for twenty years, building a portfolio of high-reliability networking products, training teams, and hardening processes. When the opportunity arrived, the company was ready.

Even so, readiness was not enough. To win large, multi-hundred-million-dollar global deals, Tejas needed more than technology. Two handicaps kept resurfacing. India was known for IT services, not high-tech products; credibility was lacking. And customers wanted to see a balance sheet that could withstand shocks. Buyers were reluctant to trust a mid-sized Indian firm with contracts that required decades of support.

The turning point came in 2021, when Tata Sons invested in Tejas. Overnight, the perception shifted. The Tata name carried global reputation for reliability, ethics, and scale. What Tejas had built patiently over two decades – through crises, reinvention, and long bets – now had the credibility of an institution behind it. The association did more than add capital. It allowed Tejas to bid for contracts that had previously been out of reach.

Within months, the impact was visible. BSNL's indigenous 4G rollout moved ahead with Tejas supplying radios and optical gear, and TCS as system integrator. The project, valued at roughly ₹7,500 crore, was executed in eighteen months – a pace claimed as the fastest 4G rollout of its scale anywhere in the world. For investors, the message was equally clear. Tejas's market valuation crossed ₹25,000 crore.

By the time the market turned in India's favor, Tejas had spent two decades preparing. Without the years of stubborn investment, the opportunity created by Galwan and unlocked by Tata would have passed. When the window finally opened, Tejas was not scrambling to catch up. It was already standing at the line, ready to deliver.

THE BONDS THAT OUTLASTED THE CRISES

Tejas Networks did not begin in a garage or over late-night conversations between friends. It began in 2000 with three co-founders who shared little history but carried complementary strengths. That mix turned out to be decisive.

Kumar, a professor at the Indian Institute of Science, was the deep-tech anchor. His textbook on optical networking had already earned global recognition. His authority came from depth, not volume; when he spoke, customers and investors listened. Arnob was the execution backbone, turning product roadmaps into

Corporate Reports

BUSINESS INDIA • August 7-20, 2000

Will Tejas light up

Brought into being by Sycamore Networks, ASG-Omni and Desh Deshpande, the new technology baby in Bangalore, Tejas Networks, aims to put India on the global hi-tech map

Bandwidth bandits: Arnob Roy, Desh Deshpande, Sanjay Nayak and Kumar Sivarajan

"Not only the three founders, more than 40% of the first two hundred employees stayed together for over twenty years."

Image credit: *Business India*

reality, assembling teams, and ensuring deadlines were met. Sanjay bridged the inside and the outside – raising funds, influencing policy, and translating market demands into product decisions. In addition he was the go-to guy for any tough-to-crack problems. From the outset, there were no overlaps and no turf wars. When their first mentor and investor, Deshpande, asked if the three could work together, the answer came without hesitation.

That clarity of roles made possible an early funding round of $5 million on day zero, even before the company had a concrete business plan. It also allowed the team to scale revenues from ₹5 crore in the first year to ₹676 crore in nine years. And when the headwinds arrived – global financial crisis, Nortel's bankruptcy, the 2G scam, floods, fire – the structure held. What carried them through was not a single technology breakthrough but shared vision, mutual respect and trust.

The same bonds extended to the larger team. Of the first two hundred employees, more than eighty stayed for over two decades, through downturns and crises. Some had returned from comfortable lives abroad because they believed in the vision of building world-class technology products from India. They stayed not for incentives but for shared purpose and loyalty forged under pressure. Investors, too, backed Tejas across volatile years, not because the numbers were always perfect, but because they trusted intent and persistence.

For a deep-tech company anywhere in the world, keeping a founding team intact for more than twenty years is rare. At Tejas, disagreements were frequent, debates fierce, but the trust in each other's strengths never broke. That trust became one of Tejas's hardest-to-replicate advantages.

By the time Sanjay stepped down in 2023, Arnob and Kumar carried the company forward. The technology, IP, and customer base were critical assets. But what truly endured was something less tangible: a culture of resilience, ethics, and loyalty, and the habit of backing one another when it was hardest to do so. That, more than any product, was Tejas's lasting legacy.

WHAT TEJAS LEFT BEHIND

From the outside, Tejas Networks looked like a telecom equipment company – optical transmission, routers, switches, base stations. But over two decades, it built something less visible and more enduring: proof that India could design and manufacture world-class technology products.

At the turn of the millennium, India was known globally as a services hub. Hardware was imported, telecom infrastructure built on foreign designs and credit. Tejas broke that pattern. Its software-defined hardware architecture gave operators flexibility and future readiness. Its products achieved the five-nines reliability that global standards demanded. By the late 2010s, every major Indian operator, public or private, was using Tejas equipment. A large share of India's critical networks – BSNL, defense, railways, power, oil and gas – ran on Tejas platforms. More than seventy-five countries around the world deployed its products.

The company's persistence also shaped policy. From preferential market access to production-linked and design-linked incentives, many of the frameworks that later supported Indian deep-tech firms drew directly from the hurdles Tejas had battled firsthand. Its manufacturing model, anchored in EMS partners like Flextronics and Sanmina, helped seed an industry that went far beyond telecom. Its funding journey – venture capital, private equity, and finally public markets – demonstrated that investors could back Indian deep-tech and find returns.

By mid-2020, when the Galwan clash forced a reckoning on foreign dependence, the groundwork had been laid. India could roll out 100,000 indigenous 4G base stations in a record eighteen months because Tejas had already proven the technology, the supply chain, and the discipline to deliver at scale.

When Sanjay stepped down in 2023, the company was bigger than its founders. Tejas had become a blueprint: how to persist through crises, how to attract and retain talent, how to build ecosystems around product companies, and how to influence national policy by example rather than rhetoric.

Today, Sanjay spends his time with entrepreneurs, investors, and policymakers, urging them to back Indian deep-tech ventures in telecom, semiconductors, and electronics. His argument is straightforward: strategic autonomy will come only when India invests in R&D, develops its own IP, and nurtures product firms that can hold their own globally.

Building a product nation takes patience, deliberate execution, and the refusal to let short-term convenience dictate long-term capability. Tejas was proof. The work now is to make that proof the norm.

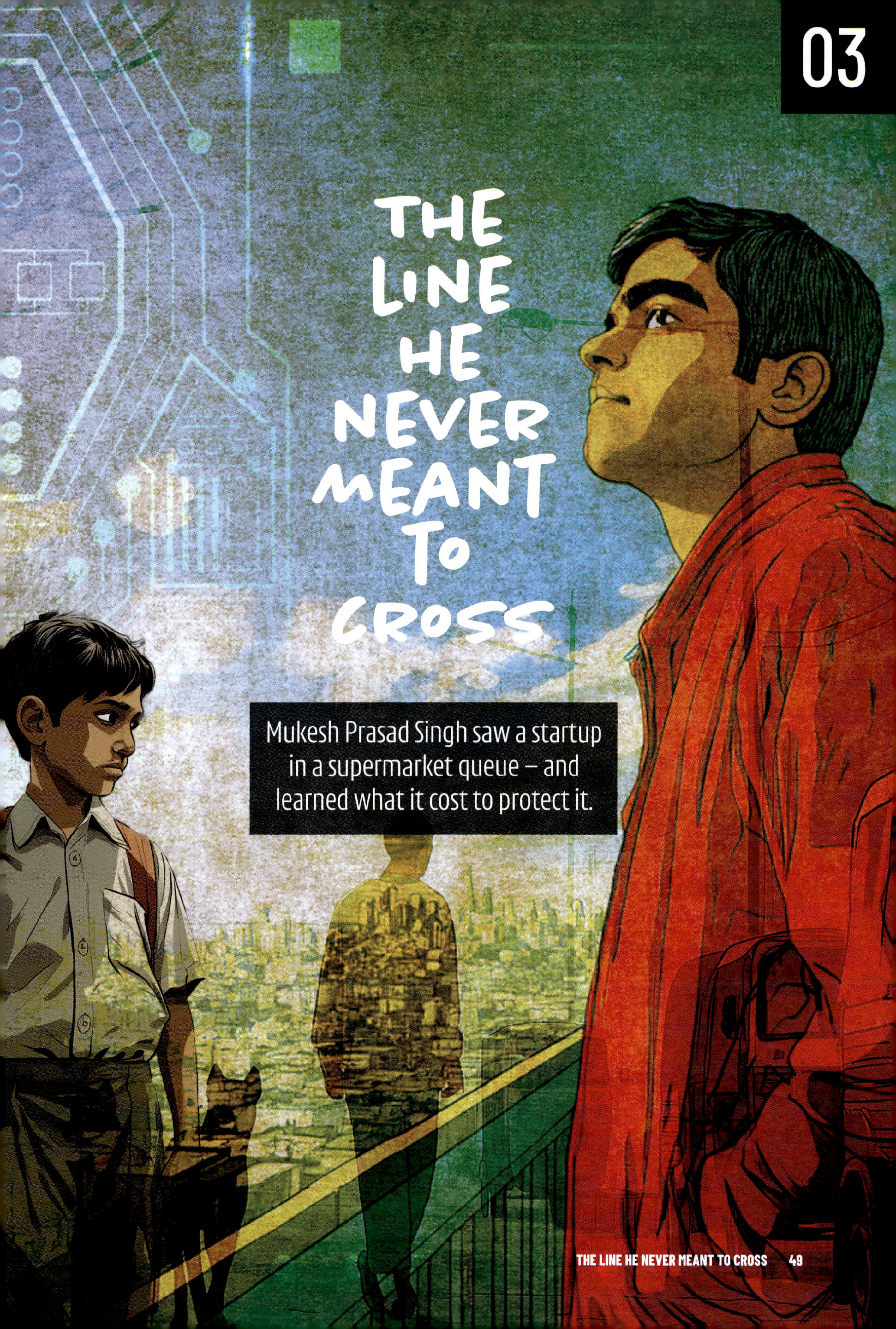

THE LINE HE NEVER MEANT TO CROSS

Mukesh Prasad Singh saw a startup in a supermarket queue – and learned what it cost to protect it.

The Five-Rupee Line

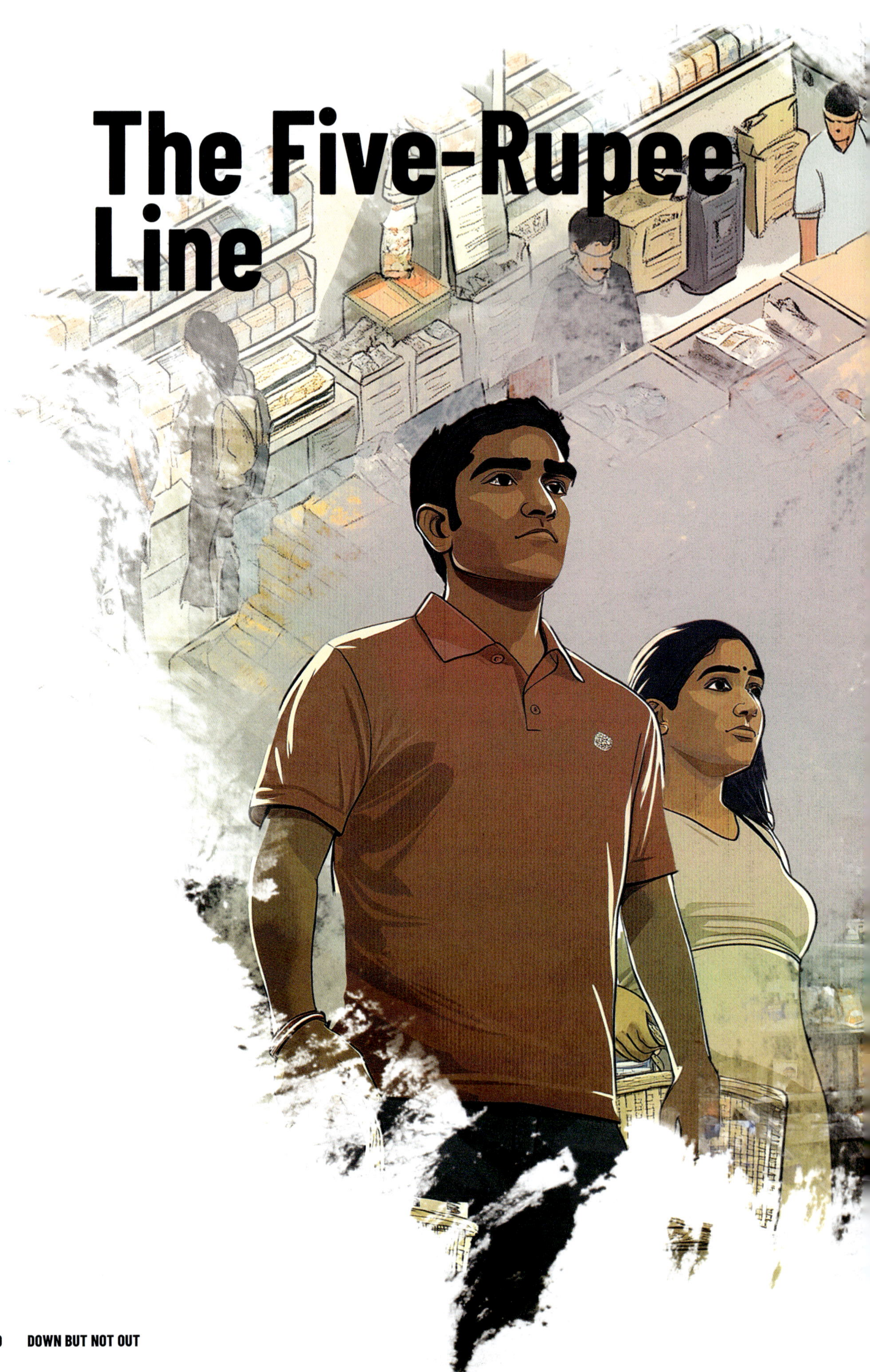

In a sweltering Gurgaon supermarket, Mukesh Prasad Singh watched a quarrel over change—and found the clarity to rebuild his life, his company, and his purpose.

PURPOSE IN A QUEUE

In April 2011, Mukesh stood with Julee, six months pregnant at the time, in the checkout line of an Easyday supermarket in Gurgaon. They were fifth or sixth in line. The man ahead was refusing to budge over five rupees the cashier didn't have. She offered him a few Eclairs toffees instead. He argued back.

Most people in that line shifted impatiently. Mukesh did not. He wasn't irritated; he was calculating. Every item in their basket – atta, dal, salt – was familiar, predictable, repeatable. He thought of Basu Aunty who ran a tiny kirana shop back in Bokaro. She used to count coins on a cloth mat each evening and repeat her refrain: *"Chhoti chhoti dikkat suljha lo. Badi aayengi hi nahin."* Take care of the small problems, the big ones won't come.

At Amazon, he had seen the same lesson institutionalized: fix small frictions first. Standing there in the stale supermarket air, he kept wondering why no one had made this process invisible. If Amazon solved harder problems every day, why not this?

It wasn't the dream of running a grocery company that seized him, it was the idea that the queue itself could disappear. More than that, it was the feeling that he wouldn't be able to walk away without trying.

Later, he would recognize the blend of instincts carried over from eGain and Amazon: win the customer by removing pain, keep them by ensuring it never returned. But that afternoon, it was simpler. He had stumbled upon a problem he couldn't unsee.

FEAR AND THE FIRST FAILURE

In Bokaro, where Mukesh grew up, hunger was not an abstract idea. It was a man – the Bhikshuk from a poem by Suryakant Tripathi 'Nirala' – his spine and stomach fused. Mukesh's father would point to him and warn, *"Padhai nahi ki toh yeh ban jaoge."* If you don't study, this will be you.

The walls in Bokaro were invisible, marked by which colony a family lived in, the books they could afford. In Bihar, where they moved to, the walls stood in plain sight. Mukesh failed the St. Xavier's entrance exam in Class 5, while his sister passed with ease. A year later he tried again, scraped through, and tasted his first failure in public.

Years later, when he cleared the JEE with rank 21, it might have felt like a triumph. But on their three-lane street, one neighbor held JEE rank #1. His best friend, Neelkanth Mishra, ranked fourth. Mukesh lived within shouting distance of them. In that environment, 21 was not special. It taught him not to chase applause.

At twenty-two years of age, living in Boston on a $1,400 fellowship at MIT, he was comfortable. Every few weeks, though, he read about some twenty-five-year-old who had become a "millionaire" through a startup. Growing up in the Indian number system, he assumed a million had five zeros. Lakhpati logic. In his head, that was enough to retire.

Soon, he took a sabbatical – technically, one he never returned from – and co-founded his first company, Zoesis. The team built interactive animation technology years ahead of its time. But in 1999, with $9 million in the bank, his co-founders wanted to run the company like a research lab. Mukesh wanted to get it into the market. He was right about the business, but too raw to convince them. He left.

For a long time, he thought the lesson was about money. That if he had stayed, he might have made more. But the real lesson was about himself. A comfortable job hid a person's edges. A startup revealed them when the ground shifted. Fear had already pushed him out of academia. Zoesis taught him how to live with risk, and how much he still had to learn.

“पेट पीठ दोनों मिलकर हैं एक”

- सूर्यकांत त्रिपाठी “निराला”

THE STARTUP THAT HELD A MIRROR

Mukesh had left MIT chasing scale. He started Zoesis chasing money.

The company folded without noise – no drama, no headlines. Just awkward goodbyes and a crumpled rent bill on his Cambridge table. What remained was the slow realization that he had been building for the wrong reason.

At MIT, he had been surrounded by people who measured themselves in millions. He thought that was what he wanted too. Zoesis had already taught him the buzz of the startup floor. Zoesis, he believed, would make him rich. When it didn't, he told himself he had failed. The truth was harder: he still didn't know what mattered to him.

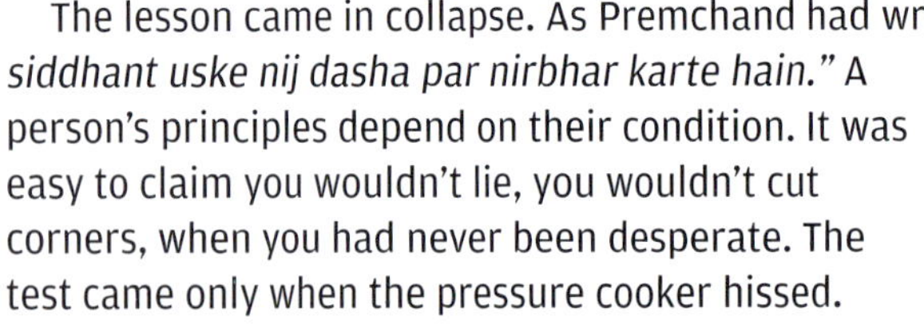

The lesson came in collapse. As Premchand had written, *"Manushya ke siddhant uske nij dasha par nirbhar karte hain."* A person's principles depend on their condition. It was easy to claim you wouldn't lie, you wouldn't cut corners, when you had never been desperate. The test came only when the pressure cooker hissed.

Zoesis put him in that cooker. He wasn't broke, but he was exposed. Without the comfort of a salary or the glow of a title, he had to face his own reflection. Two realizations cut through: money could not be the only driver, and impact mattered more than accumulation.

That shift, from money to meaning, was uncomfortable, but it endured. It was the reason he walked into Amazon later with different eyes. And it was the reason, years after Zoesis disappeared, the mirror it held up was still with him.

In a startup, the first product is yourself.

AMAZON'S TWO GIFTS

Amazon gave Mukesh two gifts that stayed with him.

The first was the power of data, not the buzzword that filled slide decks, but data as a living, breathing part of how to run a company. Every high-level meeting began with customer service complaints, not revenue. If tables were arriving broken, Jeff Bezos wanted to know why before he wanted to see sales figures. The team would run through the Five Whys until the trail led back to the packaging line, not the product. Once every quarter, regardless of title, employees spent a day in the call center, a day in the warehouse, and a day writing code. It kept them grounded. It kept the customer real.

The second was ownership. With ownership came trust, and with trust came the obligation to act when something wasn't working. Bezos once handed the AWS charter to a leader who wasn't an engineer, simply because he had the clearest business logic. That was ownership: pick the right person, then give them the space and responsibility to deliver. And if they weren't the right person, get them off the bus quickly.

Inside Amazon, OP1 and OP2 – the annual operating plans – felt exactly like fundraising rounds. You made your case, justified your spend, and delivered on your numbers or risked being shut down. It was entrepreneurial without the romance. And when things went well, the rewards were real, but never for coasting.

Those two gifts – obsession with the customer and unflinching ownership – shaped every decision Mukesh made afterwards. They were in his head years later, when he sat across from his co-founder, BK Birla and realized he would have to choose the company over the friendship. Amazon had prepared him for that moment.

THE ULTIMATUM

The travel tally at Amazon had become a metronome: eighteen international trips in fifty-two weeks, airport lounges bleeding into one another. The passport felt heavier than the suitcase. At home, Julee – resolute and steady – drew a line without raising her voice: “You can’t keep living out of suitcases, not every nine or ten days.” The words landed harder than any performance review.

Amazon had taught Mukesh discipline and scale. Julee’s sentence taught him the cost. He said later, with the same matter-of-fact clarity he brought to ops, “If you lose sight of your family, you’re just a monk.” He left Amazon in 2009. MakeMyTrip followed, Gurgaon over Seattle, fewer boarding passes over status miles. It wasn’t a leap; it was a correction. He showed up, delivered, went home. Something inside slowed, not from fatigue, but from a different kind of attention.

Then one afternoon, in a sweltering Easyday queue, a five-rupee dispute cut through the haze. Basu Aunty’s coin stacks. Bezos’s “play to our strengths.” A basket of predictable SKUs – atta, salt, dal. The thought wasn’t glamorous: make the queue disappear. The ambition wasn’t abstract: restore dignity to a daily chore. The clarity that Amazon had sharpened met the boundary Julee had set and pointed to the next thing.

Z-O-P-N-O-W

Grocery had broken the bigger players. In the U.S., the spectacular failure of Webvan proved that glowing reviews could still be buried by routes and costs; logistics unraveled despite love from customers. India, Mukesh believed, held a structural advantage Webvan never had: density. Vertical living, stacked towers, multiple deliveries an elevator ride apart. Press a few buttons and you serve a building, not a block. Efficiency might live in proximity.

The name arrived the way many usable ideas do – on a jog. An auto-rickshaw with a misspelled sign: "Zop." Online, the domain check returned eleven dollars for ZopNow.com. He bought it. Birla was skeptical until his daughter, Shristi, wrote it out on a notepad – Z-O-P-N-O-W – and made the strangeness feel obvious, workable.

What began as a fix for a five-rupee headache gathered form: build for India's density, not America's distance; design for predictability, not coupons; treat operations as a system, not a favor. The bet wasn't that grocery was easy. The bet was that in India, done a certain way, it could finally work.

THE LINE I CROSSED

For Mukesh, ZopNow was everything. For Birla, it was one of many things.

From the start, they had divided roles: Mukesh would handle investment and technology, Birla would handle marketing and operations. But operations was a 24x7 beast. When delivery boys began holding cash overnight because the process wasn't enforced, it was not a minor glitch. It was a crack in the foundation. Birla believed in trusting people. Mukesh believed in trusting processes.

He offered to swap roles. Birla refused.

By then, Mukesh had absorbed the hard lesson from Amazon: if the wrong person is on the bus, you get them off quickly. The problem was that in a startup, the "wrong person" could also be a friend who had housed you, whose daughter had helped name the company. That was when the board had to step in. Subrata listened for a month, ran their own checks, and came back clear: this could not be fixed.

They called Birla into Accel's office. The meeting lasted five minutes. Subrata delivered the decision. Mukesh wasn't in the room. He had already prepared the operations team so that deliveries would not falter the next day.

That night Birla wrote a blog. Julee learned of the split from it. In the post, Birla changed their names and laced it with anger. Mukesh never read it. He decided not to. Why carry bitterness you don't need? He told the team there would be no public replies, no counter-story. Dirty linen would not be washed in public.

They agreed on a buyout figure, which Mukesh paid from his own money. His mistake, his responsibility. The company would not suffer for his error in picking the wrong partner. Was he 50% responsible or 100%? To him, the question was pointless.

He still liked Birla. He only wished ZopNow had been Birla's "everything" too. But when a company became your baby, you crossed the line to protect it. Even if it meant losing a friend.

STARTUPS STRIP YOU BARE

After Birla left, the warehouse did not collapse. Orders went out, metrics kept moving. To the team, nothing seemed broken. But inside, Mukesh carried the weight of a fracture that blurred friendship and survival.

He had once lived in Birla's home. He had played with their children. Birla's daughter had helped name the company. And yet he had been forced to see that same friend as a threat to his startup, and to act accordingly.

At night, when the warehouse quieted, guilt entered. Mukesh replayed the scenes: the refusal to swap roles, the argument over cash handling, the brief five-minute dismissal at Accel. But he carried doubt. Was he too rigid? Too controlling? Had his insistence on processes over people stripped the warmth out of ZopNow?

At home, the cost was sharper in its silence. Julee and Naman absorbed his absence without complaint. That silence pressed harder than any confrontation. "It's easier to fight anger," he thought, "than to accept grace."

Years later, when asked, he would distill the experience into a single truth: "Startups strip you bare. You never meet these sides of yourself when life is comfortable. You meet them only when survival puts someone you love on the other side of the line."

Between 2016 and 2018, that stripping happened again. ZopNow was in doldrums. The market wanted growth at all costs, preferably discount-driven. Mukesh refused to turn his company into a coupon circus.

The consequences were brutal. They lost some of their best people to higher salaries. He didn't blame them; if someone offered five times the pay, you went. Still, it hurt to watch them leave. He kept the company afloat with his own money. Two million dollars set aside for family safety was untouchable. Beyond that, everything went in.

The harder part wasn't the money. It was the uncertainty. Risk was when you knew the odds. Uncertainty was when you didn't. For two years he woke up not knowing if the company would still exist in six months, but also knowing the technology they had built was valuable. They just hadn't figured out how to monetize it.

At home, the weight deepened. Their family didn't take the trips others posted about. Julee and Naman never complained, which somehow made it worse.

Seven years of running groceries had been the test. ZopSmart was the scale. The baby survived. So did Mukesh. But he aged more in those two years than in the ten before them.

BE READY WHEN THE MUSIC STARTS

One evening at his childhood friend Neelkanth's home, the talk turned from memories to business. Casually, Neelkanth said, "I'm meeting B.S. Nagesh tomorrow. Come along." Nagesh was the chairman of Shoppers Stop.

The invitation shifted more than it seemed. Weeks later, ZopNow was piloting inside a HyperCity store in Bangalore. For Mukesh, it felt like the perfect A/B test: density in action, delivery distances collapsing, logistics suddenly within reach.

The optimism didn't last. Digital inventory rarely matched what sat on the shelves. Orders went out incomplete, customers grew frustrated, and every complaint landed on him. He had promised predictability. The system was failing it.

Mukesh turned frustration into code. Drawing from the playbook he had absorbed at Amazon, he pushed his engineers toward predictive analytics – not reports for dashboards, but algorithms designed to see demand before the customer asked. Over time, the mismatches narrowed. Inventory accuracy improved, delivery reliability steadied, and trust slowly returned.

The lesson hardened into conviction. For Mukesh, technology wasn't about efficiency alone. It was about restoring dignity to the everyday act of shopping. HyperCity proved a larger truth: survival depended less on raising capital and more on the discipline and systems a company built for itself. And it reminded him of something he carried from the start. Entrepreneurship was an unpredictable dance with serendipity. The only job was to be ready when the music began.

GRACEFUL WIND-DOWN

ZopNow didn't end in a crash. Mukesh landed it, systems intact, lessons banked, so the useful parts could fly again.

For years he had invested in one core: an omnichannel stack built to gain and sustain customers – site and app, inventory and warehouse control, picking, packing, last-mile. While investors pushed grow, grow, grow, he kept to Amazon's rulebook: start with the customer, own the outcome. When the partnership broke, he took the hit himself and paid the buyout from personal funds.

Then came 2016–18. Funding cooled, talent left, and he fed the business with his own money, keeping a $2 million family buffer untouched. He refused to turn ZopNow into a coupon circus; the offer was convenience, not discounts. It wasn't risk – there were no odds to price. It was uncertainty.

The turn arrived outside him. As Amazon moved on Whole Foods, overnight, omnichannel went from nice-to-have to must-have. Retailers now wanted what his team had been building since 2011. ZopNow, the consumer brand, could end with dignity. ZopSmart – the engine beneath it – could scale.

He even marked the shift in himself, retiring a patriotic email sign-off to widen the frame: build for the world, not just at home.

The brand wound down. The stack went to work.

THE LONGEST RUN

Mukesh Prasad Singh still runs.

Not for pace. Not for medals. Because it's the only time he hears himself clearly.

The world of quick commerce he once imagined now moves at ten-minute speed. VC decks cheer delivery bikes; ten-minute grocery is sold as freedom. He scrolls past the headlines, not bitter – just precise. ZopNow wasn't wrong. It was early. Maybe too early.

Sometimes he wonders: would it have landed differently if he'd exited at the peak, if the story had ended in noise instead of fatigue? He doesn't dwell. That was never the point.

He isn't building right now. He's pausing. There's a teenager at home with only a few more years under this roof. A wife whose silence taught him more about consequence than any investor memo ever could. Most mornings, he ties his laces beside Naman. Sometimes they run together. Sometimes he runs alone.

On those runs, the old anchors return. Nirala's Bhikshuk – spine and stomach fused in warning.

Basu Aunty stacking coins on a cloth mat: solve the small problems and the big ones won't come.

Other lessons surface too.

Amazon's two gifts: data that begins with the customer, ownership that doesn't flinch.

The monk line after eighteen trips in fifty-two weeks: if you lose sight of your family, you're just a monk.

India's density over America's distance.

A misspelled "Zop" on an auto.

He didn't solve every problem. But he saw them early. He tried, built, bled – and when it mattered, he paused. The Easyday queue never really left him, because it wasn't only a broken system; it was a harder question: Who do you become when no one is watching?

Mukesh crossed the line to find out. He's still running – not from something, not toward something – with something that refuses to let go.

"Ek aisa sach jisse sab bhaagte hain. Aur main uske peeche bhaag raha hoon." (A truth everyone runs from. And I'm running toward it.)

NOT DEAD, JUST NOT DONE

BlueStone nearly died. Gaurav Singh Kushwaha refused to walk away.

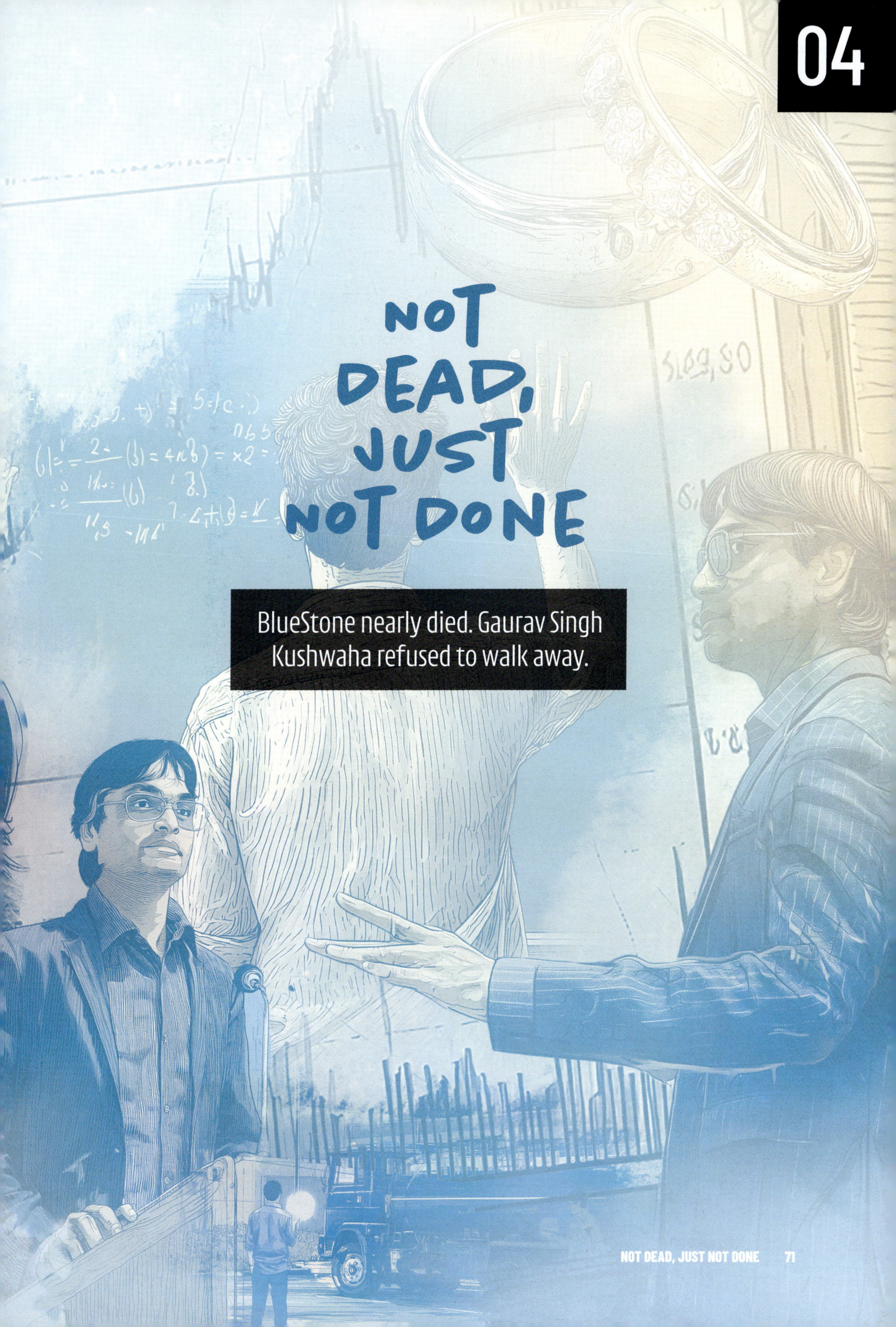

WHEN FAILURE ISN'T LOUD

Early 2017. The BlueStone office in Bangalore had the hollow feel of a place that used to be full.

A few months earlier, about 150 people worked here. After the cuts, only twenty remained. Five were engineers. There was no one in marketing or product. Birthdays had been celebrated at the long central table, post-lunch chai carried on in small groups near the windows. Now, there was only the faint hum of the ceiling fan and the smell of stale coffee in abandoned mugs.

Gaurav Singh sat at his desk with a spreadsheet open on his laptop. Each row was a name. Not abstract entries, but people he had recruited, worked alongside, joked with. Many had joined in BlueStone's early rise, leaving more stable jobs because they believed in the story he'd told them. Now the same names were numbers in a downsizing column.

The decision had been weeks in the making. The company's burn rate had outpaced revenue for too long. Marketing had already been cut to zero. Product development had slowed to a crawl. Investors were polite in meetings but had stopped asking questions that signalled continued belief. Peers in the startup circuit – some of whom had once sought his advice on SEO and early traction – now spoke of him, if at all, in the softened past tense reserved for "good guys who didn't make it."

The math was clear: BlueStone could not survive without a dramatic reduction in headcount. But no formula on the spreadsheet could blunt the fact that each line represented someone whose livelihood would change by the end of the day.

Gaurav decided there would be no HR template emails, no collective announcement. He would speak to each person himself. "It was important to say it face to face," he recalled later. "To make sure they knew, it wasn't their mistake. It was ours."

He stood, carrying the first name in his mind. The floor was almost too quiet; the faint tap of his shoes on tile felt loud. Past the whiteboard still marked with curling Diwali decorations. Past desks with potted plants that would not be watered again. Past a wall that had once been dense with Post-Its, now mostly bare.

In the small conference room, he delivered the news. No euphemisms. No spin. Just the truth: "It's not your fault. It's ours." Some nodded quickly. Others avoided eye contact. One young engineer, who had joined less than a year earlier, shook his hand and said softly, "Still proud to have built with you." That one almost broke him.

One by one, the conversations continued. Near the coffee

machine, by the bookshelf with its worn carpet patch, and in the corners where the team had once crowded around a laptop for a new product demo. By lunch, desks were being cleared. By evening, the office was nearly empty.

When he sat down again, the spreadsheet was still open. The number at the bottom of the column had dropped to six. Six people left: four engineers plus Sudeep and Sameer, who had stayed without conditions.

There was no relief. Only a sharper silence. The kind that doesn't just hang in the air but settles into the body. The kind you carry home.

That night, Gaurav closed the laptop and turned off the office lights. Something had ended. But something else – harder to name – had begun: a decision to keep going, even when almost everything that made it feel like a company was gone.

Years later, when asked about that day, he didn't speak about strategy or recovery. He spoke about the act itself: "If you start throwing people at problems, you stop understanding them. We were down to six people, and that's when we really started fixing things."

For BlueStone, and for him, the rebuilding began in that stripped-down silence. Ledger by ledger.

THE PUZZLE-SOLVER MINDSET

Gaurav Singh Kushwaha grew up in Dadabari, Kota, in a one-room home with his elder brother and parents. His father worked at the local branch of UCO Bank, formal shirt and trousers every day, nine to six. It was not a business family. Diligence was picked up by watching.

At Bansal Classes in Kota, the lecture halls were packed with aspirants, but Gaurav was not the loudest. He noticed things others missed. In one physics class, the teacher wrote a solution on the blackboard. It looked complete. Gaurav raised his hand. "This doesn't work," he said. The teacher checked, then nodded. He was right.

That exactness stayed with him. He cleared the IIT entrance while recovering from a foot injury. On the counselling day, floods stopped him from reaching IIT Bombay. He enrolled at IIT Delhi instead.

His first job took him to Germany. The first paycheck, in Deutsche Mark, felt unreal. More lasting was the way an early manager worked. Instead of giving instructions, he asked questions until the answer became clear. "He never pushed," Gaurav said. "But somehow I'd always end up seeing it his way."

Back in Bangalore, his flatmates included Amit Jain and Vineet Rao. By the late 2000s he was watching how entertainment networks in the U.S. turned

ratings and comments into habit. India had no such product. He reconnected with his IIT classmate Nitin. Together they started Chakpak, a movie-focused social network. They learned how to use Google's PageRank and, for a while, outran larger players in search. But traffic did not turn into money. The internet in India was not ready. Growth stalled.

They sold the company to Flipkart at a distress price. Investors got some of their money back. The founders did not. What Gaurav carried was simpler: a decision not to stop the next time. "The desire not to fail again," he said.

After Chakpak there was no quick restart. He stayed with his brother in Delhi, then moved back to Bangalore into a rented flat in Koramangala. He read, thought through ideas, and looked back at what had gone wrong. Too much guesswork. Too little proof. "I told myself I wouldn't build like that again."

For him, problems were never about drama. They were problems to be worked through step by step, like puzzles. Whether it was a wrong equation on a blackboard, a mentor guiding him through questions in Germany, or the slow collapse of Chakpak, he treated each the same way: observe, gather the pieces, and keep at it until they fit.

That habit stayed. Years later, whether it was rebuilding BlueStone's accounting files, answering customers himself, or holding back in meetings so others could reach the answer, the approach was the same: treat it like a puzzle, and solve.

THE FADE-OUT

Chakpak didn't end suddenly. It slowed down until it stopped.

The graphs on the wall didn't dip; they just stopped climbing. In the beginning, Gaurav and Nitin believed the social layer they were building for Indian movies was inevitable – IMDb meets Facebook, but for Bollywood. They went deep into how Google's PageRank worked and turned it into an edge. If you searched for Aishwarya Rai, Salman Khan, or Shah Rukh Khan in 2007, Chakpak showed up on the first page.

The expertise made them teachers as well as founders. "Sachin and Binny would come over to learn SEO from us," Gaurav said. "Myntra's early guys too. TutorVista, CarDekho – all of them." For a while, Chakpak was the company others came to for visibility.

Traffic was not the problem. Millions of visits came in. The problem was money. Ad rates were too low. Payments were rare. E-commerce was barely starting. They could drive traffic, but they could not turn it into revenue.

Inside the company, the mood shifted. Meetings ran longer and led nowhere. Decisions lost their edge. Some people left. Others stayed on, weighed down by fatigue. "People go into panic attacks," Gaurav said. "People go into depression, technical depression also. We went through that."

The sale to Flipkart happened without any announcements or celebrations. The price was a fraction of what they had once imagined. Investors got some money back; the founders did not. "Not that we made money," Gaurav said. "But we returned significant money to the investors." He didn't call it a win. What stayed with him was simpler: "The desire not to stop next time. To not fail again."

Afterward, he did not start again immediately. He moved to Delhi and lived with his brother. The startup world moved on quickly – new rounds, new names, new headlines. His was spoken of in the past tense, if at all. There was no secret plan, no next pitch. Just time spent waiting.

Later, back in Bangalore, he rented a flat in Koramangala. Flipkart was expanding rapidly, visible all over the city, but he was outside it. He read, mapped ideas, and looked back at what had gone wrong. Too much belief. Too little counting. Too many things left untested.

He told himself he would not build like that again. The next company would have real margins, measurable trust, and systems that worked even if the market turned away. Chakpak ended without fanfare, but it gave him a hard rule: endurance had to be built in from the start.

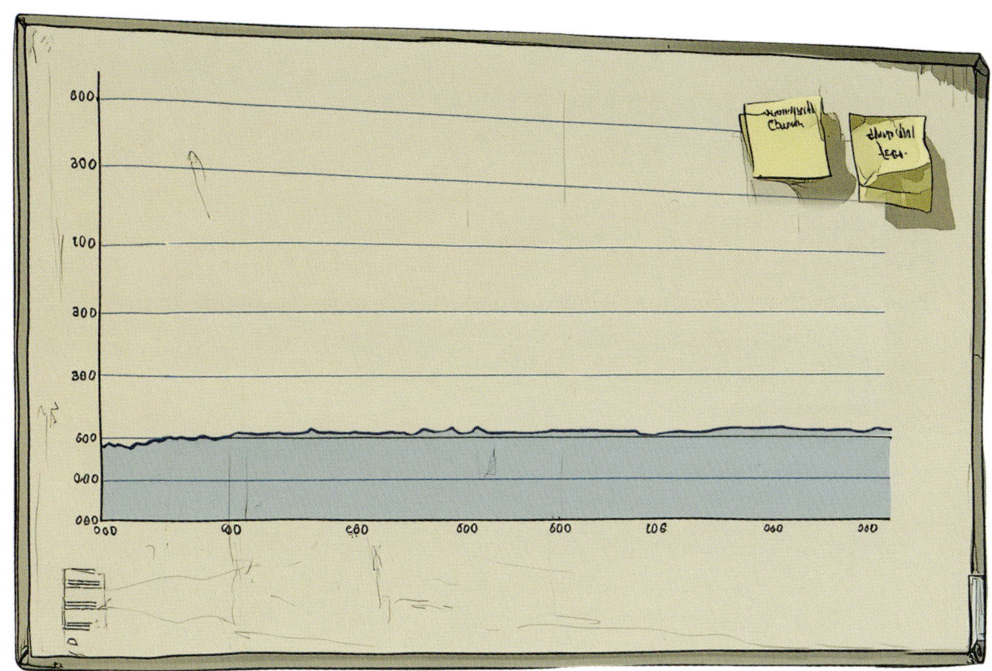

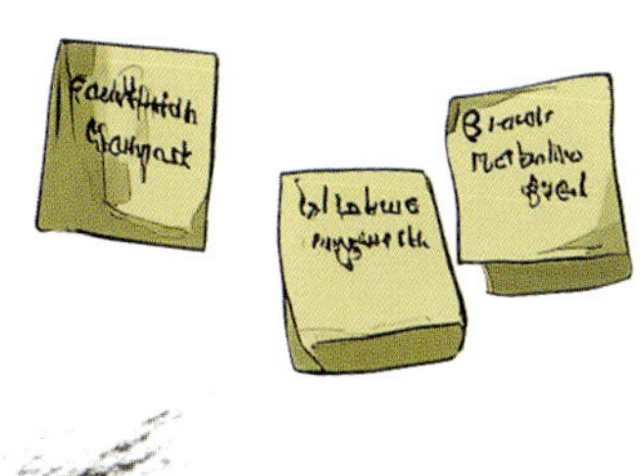

AN OUTSIDER IN GOLD

BlueStone began with a connection. Ganesh Krishnan, who had advised Gaurav during Chakpak, introduced him to Vidya Nataraj, who wanted to build a jewelry venture. By late 2011, Accel had already written a check – about $4 million. The company was incorporated. A launch was slated for March 2012.

Four to six months in, Vidya left. Gaurav was left holding a funded company that had to be built. "It's like a child is born – you have to raise it," he said later.

He was not a jewelry founder. "I had never even stepped inside a jewelry store," he admitted. "I wasn't married. I had no clue about the category." The industry treated him as an outsider who could be taken advantage of.

The early model relied on job-workers around the city. They handled casting, setting, finishing. The work came back late and inconsistent. Delivery times stretched to three or four weeks. Specifications were off. A ring listed at five grams often came back at six, or at four-and-a-half. Visual details shifted too – petal counts, stone placements. "Standard deviation was around 20-25%," Gaurav said. The assumption was that these naïve techies wouldn't notice.

Within eight to ten months he decided dependence on job-workers had to end. He and Sudeep, who had joined by then, rented a small room in Marol, Mumbai. They set up a casting bench and hired two diamond setters. From there, BlueStone began making its own pieces.

That was the company's real start. With control of the line, deviations came down to ±2%. Turnaround times dropped from weeks to three days. Sudeep anchored factory operations. Sameer, who had once taken the unusual step of joining a jeweler in Ahmedabad straight out of IIM, became the domain bridge, translating the industry's shorthand and guiding vendor negotiations.

From Marol, the operation scaled. By late 2013 they had moved to Jaipur. The facility there grew into one of the largest in the city, a backbone capable of supporting hundreds of stores.

Gaurav never claimed mastery of the trade. "I still can't run the factory myself," he said. But between him, Sudeep, and Sameer, the team had covered design, operations, manufacturing, and retail. The outsider stayed long enough to become part of the industry not by inheritance, but by building the system piece by piece.

6.00g ±2%

THE PERCEPTION FUNERAL

By 2016, the online-only model had stopped scaling. Burn was ₹7-8 crore a month. Orders weren't growing fast enough. Stores were delayed. Payroll had swelled to a size the company couldn't carry. In early 2017, the reckoning arrived.

That was the morning of the spreadsheet. Rows of names, one by one, became conversations that ended with an apology. From about 150 people in the Bangalore office, only twenty remained. Five were engineers. There was no one in marketing or product.

The layoffs were not the end, but they began the hardest stretch – when perception itself shifted.

Investor meetings still happened, but the tone was different. The questions were careful. The smiles polite. The eyes steady, but already elsewhere. "There was a time," Gaurav said, "you could see it in everyone's eyes that we were being written off."

In the press, BlueStone's name barely appeared. In Bangalore cafés, on WhatsApp groups, at meetups, the chatter was about others – companies raising large rounds, opening new markets, hiring at speed. BlueStone surfaced only as a polite afterthought, if at all.

Inside the office, there was no choice but to keep going. The team could sit around one table. Gaurav was back to running Facebook Ads himself, writing copy, tweaking targeting, fixing broken links so orders could move through. There were no growth managers, no agencies, no marketing team. Every rupee mattered. Payroll was a week-to-week calculation.

One rejection cut deeper than the rest: an investment committee "no" from a fund led by a batchmate. After the call, Gaurav couldn't sleep for three nights. But even that passed into the same rhythm – debugging campaigns, answering customers, making it through the week.

He didn't fight perception with PR. He didn't lobby for panels or news coverage. The energy went into patching systems, keeping customers, and staying solvent long enough to matter again.

Irrelevance proved a colder threat than failure. Failure is loud, final, sometimes even clarifying. Irrelevance is slow. It lets you keep moving while closing the space around you. Those years taught him that survival wasn't about proving anyone wrong in public. It was about refusing, in private, to agree that they were right.

ROLLING BACK TO SURVIVE

By 2017-18, BlueStone was in what Gaurav later called its hardest period – tougher even than the collapse of Chakpak.

The online-only model had flatlined. Traffic and transactions were not growing. Physical stores, which he believed were essential for scale, were still months away. Costs had risen on the assumption that momentum would close the gap. Money had run out.

"We were very clear," he said. "Online only is not going to scale significantly. Stores were still some time away. Costs had already ballooned. And we had run out of money. I didn't want to burn even a single rupee without a reason."

So he pulled revenues down deliberately. Instead of chasing growth, he cut online campaigns to the minimum. "Just for the sake of it, I didn't want to grow online," he said. The top line fell further. Layoffs continued. "You are firing people all to reduce costs so that you have enough left in your pocket by the time you open your stores."

What remained was skeletal. Engineering went from about forty people to four. Marketing was one person: him. The monthly manpower bill dropped from ₹7-8 crore to about ₹1.2 crore. There was no finance team. No mid-layer of managers. Just Gaurav, Sudeep in the factory, and Sameer holding retail.

It wasn't a pivot. It wasn't reinvention. It was harsher than that: a rollback to the last state the company had worked in. "Let's go back to the state where it was working," he told himself. Everything added in 2016 – expensive hires, middle management, processes copied from other funded companies – was stripped out.

Investors did not want to hear this story. But it kept the company alive. And it gave Gaurav a principle that stayed with him: survival comes from first principles, not from borrowed playbooks.

A CATEGORY YOU CAN COUNT

When Ganesh Krishnan and Vidya Nataraj asked him to join their online jewelry venture, Gaurav didn't say yes because he understood the category. He said yes because it met the rule he had set for himself after Chakpak: pick a business with real margins, control the variables, avoid guesswork.

From the start, one decision was fixed: BlueStone would not be a marketplace. "Fine jewelry doesn't work as a marketplace," Gaurav said. "The level of trust needed is very high. The value of variety is very low. You don't want two million rings. You want twenty good ones."

They launched with about three hundred designs – half developed in-house, half bought from manufacturer catalogs. The first crisis came immediately: they could not photograph the products well enough to sell them. Twenty days of shoots made the gold look fake and the stones flat. "One guy said, 'I'll touch up in Photoshop'," Gaurav recalled. "I told him – then why did we even shoot them?"

The fix came from work he had done years earlier. At Chakpak, and even before that, he had built games on Facebook using 3D assets. If people were willing to pay $25 for a virtual castle in FarmVille, he reasoned, then a ring could be rendered to look real.

He brought in the same skills. Every piece was modelled in 3D and rendered under a controlled system: same background, same lighting, same angle. Customers could rotate and zoom. A five-gram ring photographed inconsistently might look wrong; rendered, it looked the same every time.

The uniformity mattered. "We were selling images," he said. "And trust needed uniformity."

Early data confirmed the effect. Design was what drove purchases – not price, not convenience. "Eighty-six percent of buyers said they bought because of the design," Gaurav said.

But the renders solved only part of the problem. The team noticed that some visitors were spending minutes, even hours, on the site: browsing fifteen, twenty, sometimes thirty pages of designs, then leaving without buying. They called these users to ask why.

The answers repeated. First: they wanted to touch and feel the jewelry before committing. Second: they wanted confidence in servicing if a stone came loose or a ring needed resizing. Third: they wanted the option to exchange or upgrade later, the way families did with their neighborhood jeweler.

Online, those assurances weren't built in. The renders created a clean, consistent aisle. What was missing was everything that came after – the part of the relationship a physical store still carried.

NO PLAYBOOK, JUST WORK

By 2016, the gap was obvious. The calls to deep browsers had revealed why: they wanted to touch the jewelry before committing, have confidence in service, and know it could be exchanged or upgraded later.

Opening a store was not a shift to traditional retail. It was a way to close that trust gap. Pacific Mall in Delhi offered space. There was no flagship strategy or launch playbook. They took what they got.

Even that ran into delays. The mall did not allow daytime construction. The flooring crew worked nights – until one night they refused, saying there was no water to mix cement. Days were slipping. Gaurav and Sameer rented a tanker, drove it to the mall themselves, and stood with flashlights while it reversed into the service bay. “We gave it to them ourselves,” Gaurav said. “Told them, now go do it.”

The store opened with about ₹1-1.5 crore worth of inventory. Sparse but organized. The branding was clean. The aim was not spectacle. It was to see whether online browsers would buy once they could try the pieces. They did. “The store just solved the last piece,” Gaurav said.

From there, rollout followed a practical rhythm. Chandigarh, Mohali, and other cities came next. The choice of sites wasn’t about prestige malls; it was about economics and availability. The franchise model was reversed: BlueStone ran the stores, franchisees funded them. Early partners were cousins, friends, past colleagues – people who already trusted Gaurav and his team.

By 2019, they had fifteen stores. It was not a rapid scale. It was a repeatable way to close the loop between online curiosity and offline trust, while keeping control of brand, operations, and the capital cycle.

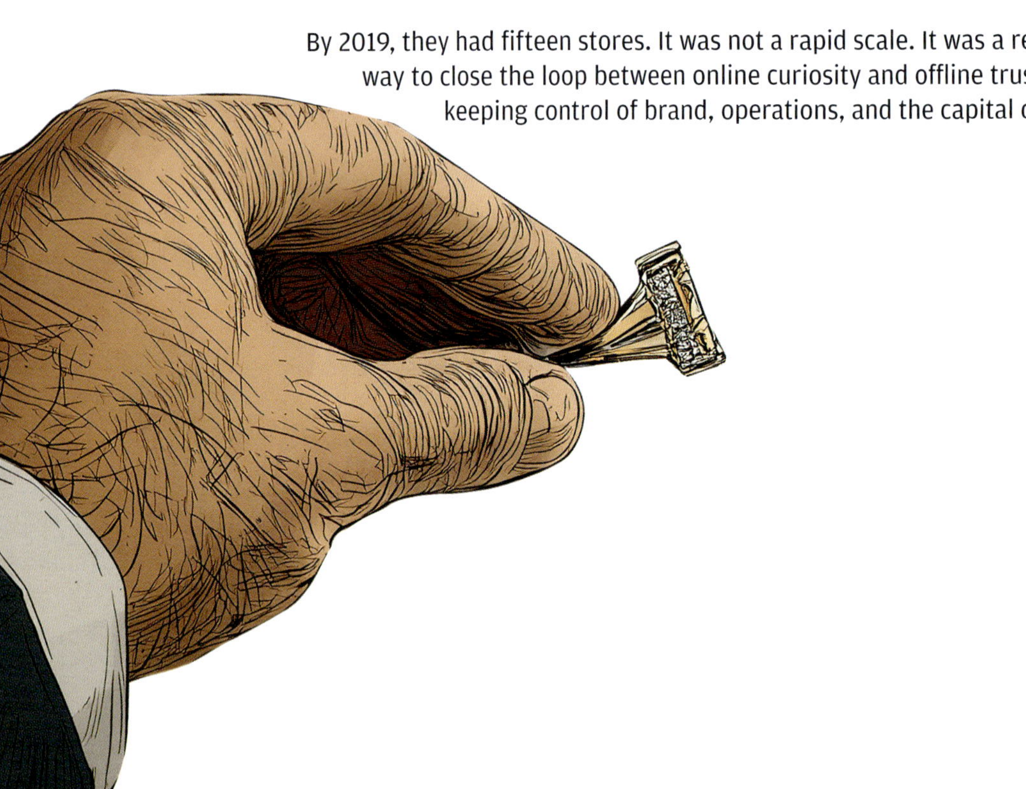

BLUESTONE
BLUESTONE

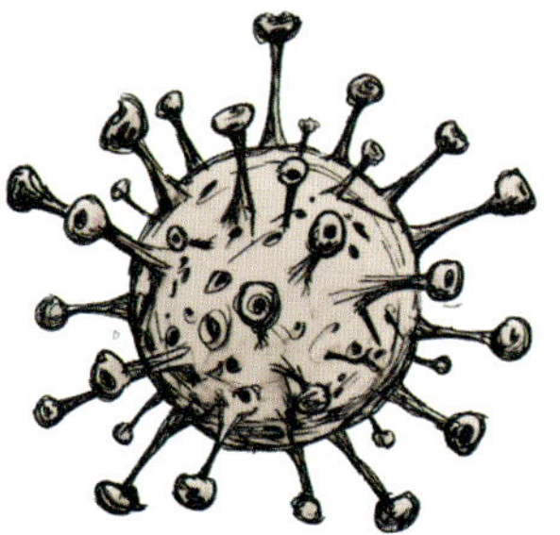

ONE HARD DECISION

By February 2020, BlueStone was steady but thin. Sixteen stores were running. The franchise model had freed up some capital. Design and merchandizing systems were working without constant founder oversight. A new funding round was in process; investor calls were regular, though slower than before.

Then Covid began edging into India's headlines. Investors grew cautious. Responses stretched from days to weeks. When the lockdown came, it was abrupt: shutters down on every store, online orders freezing within days.

The immediate danger wasn't lost revenue. It was the company's financing structure. Most of BlueStone's gold was held through gold metal loans – efficient in normal times because they conserved working capital. But in a crisis, they carried a sharp risk. If gold prices spiked, banks could demand more margin money immediately. That meant parking more cash in fixed deposits against the loan – cash BlueStone didn't have.

At the time, reserves were about ₹4-6 crore. Enough for a couple of months, not for sudden multi-crore calls. And gold, as it always does in a crisis, was climbing.

The choice was clear. Keep the hedge and risk a fatal call from the bank, or break it – close the position, absorb the risk of swings in the open market, and keep the cash.

"Break the hedge. Protect cash first," Gaurav told his team. On paper, it could have backfired badly if gold prices fell. But the larger danger was being wiped out overnight by a margin call. The hedge was closed. The cash stayed in the bank.

Days later, a second blow landed. A $5 million commitment that had been in final paperwork collapsed overnight. The reason from one LP (Limited Partner) was blunt: "Luxury is dead."

There was no time to argue. Gaurav called the people who had seen BlueStone through worse. Prashanth Prakash. Sameer Nath. The bridge money came without decks or rounds of meetings. Just short confirmations: "Will wire tomorrow - P." / "We're in."

The months that followed were survival work: converting some stores to franchisee-owned formats to cut lease costs, negotiating rent deferrals, keeping operations at the minimum. The hedge break never appeared in public updates. But inside the company, it became a marker. Not a vision statement. Not strategy. Just a decision that meant the difference between dying in days or living to fight again.

Will wire tomorrow
We’re in.
Confirm Hedge Close
Yes
No

ANCHORS IN THE HARD YEARS

BlueStone didn't make it through its hardest stretch because of a system or a strategy. It made it because people stayed when it would have been easier to leave.

The Founder on the Frontlines

During the leanest months, customer escalations carried real risk. A ring that didn't fit, a clasp that broke, a delivery missed before a wedding – any of these could undo trust in a business where trust was already fragile. Most founders would have passed those calls down. Gaurav didn't. He answered them himself – on LinkedIn, by email, often at night.

"You can be completely correct according to your SOP," he said, "and still be completely wrong in the customer's eyes."

He stopped defending. He apologized – not because the company was always at fault, but because the inconvenience was real. Over time, that instinct spread into the company: return policies softened, processes bent toward empathy.

Sudeep Nagar: The Invisible Owner

When the company shrank to the bone, Sudeep carried what in a larger firm would have been three different roles. He ran factory floors, pushed store openings, rewired ERPs, negotiated leases, kept operations running end to end.

"We cut our manpower bill from 7-8 crore to 1.2 crore," Gaurav said. "At that time, everything – opening stores, building systems, running the factory – it was just the two of us."

When BlueStone began hiring CXOs again, there was a risk his role would disappear into hierarchy. Elevating him to co-founder was not a reward. It was to make visible what was already gravity. "It's not about power," Gaurav said. "It's about gravity. People need to know who anchors what."

Sameer Gandhi: The Jewelry Bridge

Sameer was another constant. An IIT junior, later an IIM graduate, he had once taken the unusual step of joining a jeweler in Ahmedabad. That meant when BlueStone was still improvising with job-workers, he was one of the few who had seen a factory from the inside. He knew whom to call, how vendors gamed outsiders, what to check.

"Between the three of us," Gaurav said, "we had covered almost every aspect of the business."

Prashanth Prakash: Neck on the Line

And then there was Prashanth Prakash. He wasn't just an investor. When rounds stalled and "luxury is dead" became shorthand for why BlueStone couldn't be funded, he kept committing – sometimes his own capital, often pulling others in.

"Six months, we'd need two million more," Gaurav said. "Prashanth would be the first to commit from Accel. Then he would go to other investors, rally them for 100k, 200k each. He put his own neck on the line."

At times, he was fighting his own internal partnerships to keep BlueStone afloat. He stayed close, guided not by consensus but by signals he trusted. Years later, at the IPO, he opened his speech with a line that summed it up: "Nothing about BlueStone is without drama."

AFTER THE BELL, STILL HOLDING

For fourteen years, every conversation around BlueStone carried the same undertone. Investors didn't just fund the company; they expected an exit. Sometimes the word was spoken directly. Other times it sat in the background – IPO, sale, liquidity. The rhythm was constant.

When BlueStone finally listed, Gaurav felt something he hadn't prepared for. It wasn't a triumph. It wasn't financial relief. He hadn't sold a single share. His own balance was unchanged. But the noise was gone.

"The completion happened," he said. "For investors, for that conversation that has been running for fourteen years. And because of that, I felt light."

He spoke that day about another weight too: the disbelief they had carried from the beginning. "We were just a bunch of engineers who knew nothing about jewelry, nothing about retail, nothing about manufacturing," he reminded the room. He remembered the first time they touched hundred orders in a single day. "That day, the feeling of disbelief turned into reality. Today I feel the same. The scale is different, the numbers are different, but the feeling is the same."

People had once dismissed the idea outright. "How can anyone buy jewelry online? Jewelry requires trust. This will never work." His reply, years later, was simple: "Why can't a new brand become a legacy, if it earns love, one customer at a time?"

He named the pillars that made it possible. Investors who backed conviction when there was no proof. A team that began as learners, failed often, and still showed up the next day. Families who gave up weekends, holidays, stability. He spoke of his wife as the "bright force" who had lived the journey alongside him from the beginning.

The morning after the listing, he went back to his desk. The work was the same. Emails stacked up. Franchise calls were scheduled. Designers pitched new collections. But the terms had shifted.

"Now I'm running this for customers and shareholders," he said. "Not for anyone else's timeline."

Gaurav remembered the first day they crossed a hundred orders. The feeling then – what looked unlikely becoming real – was the same.

BlueStone's listing wasn't a payday. It ended an obligation that wasn't his alone. What remained: the company, the customers, and the people who stayed.

NEWS
BLUESTONE: LISTED
NSE

05

NOT THE TWELFTH MAN

This is the story of a founder unwilling to be the twelfth man in life. Willing to bleed on the field, lose, get back up, and keep chasing. For Raghu, entrepreneurship is unfinished by design.

The End That Wasn't Closure

In March 2015, Raghu told two hundred employees the end had come, then signed away TaxiForSure in the office where it began.

THE VOID OF A "SUCCESSFUL" EXIT

On March 15, 2015, the TaxiForSure sale was officially done. Less than five years old, the company had raised about $12 million and delivered a $200 million cash exit. In the lens of Indian startups at the time, it was historic. After redBus and Myntra, it was the rare early cash-out. Investors saw it as one of the cleanest returns of the era.

Raghu felt none of the triumph.

"Something was taken away from me," he says. "Till then, I would wake up and only think about TaxiForSure. After the exit, there was a void."

The transaction that made him wealthy brought only turmoil. "We never did it for money," he says. "We had to do it for employees, because of drivers, because of customers, because of investors. Failure was never an option. We did it for others."

What stung more was who sat across the table. "And that too it was Ola, a rival. We had to take it with a pinch of salt."

For the outside world, it was cause for celebration. Batchmates and classmates called to congratulate him. Investors sent notes of felicitation. "Everybody thinks it was a successful exit," Raghu remembers. "But I felt thrown away from the ecosystem."

Even the days immediately after were consumed not by relief, but by bureaucracy. The deal closed in mid-March; by March 30, wealth managers were pressing him about tax filings. "That kept me busy for fifteen days," he says. "Then the void returned."

He struggled to understand whom to share the feeling with. "Who would understand? To everyone else, it looked like a triumph. A great exit, money in the bank. But to me, it felt unfinished, as though my journey had been cut short."

For Raghu, the absence was not just about what was lost, but about what never arrived. Closure. "Closures are individual," he says. "It's not what the rest of the world thinks. For me, there was no closure with TFS."

In those weeks, he understood the solitude of the founder. "Nobody cares what the founder is going through," he says. "Everybody takes care of themselves. The founder has to take care of everyone else. It is a lonely journey for a founder."

He recognizes he was among the lucky ones: at least his exit was on the "positive side of the money flow." Many others in the same position saw their companies collapse without return. Yet even that perspective could not blunt the void.

For the ecosystem, TaxiForSure was a celebrated chapter closed. For Raghu, it was an unfinished story and the beginning of a haunting search for what came next.

THE MAKING OF RAGHU

Raghu grew up in South Bangalore, Basavanagudi side, in a middle-class home: father in state government, mother a homemaker. Three siblings: an elder sister just a year ahead of him, then Raghu, then a younger brother. All three studied computer science: his sister at PESIT (today an IPS officer, Karnataka cadre; currently a director at the National Police Academy), Raghu at NITK Suratkal, his brother at an engineering college in Mysore before moving to the U.S.

The extended family lived in a tight cluster of homes – even intertwined marriages (his father's two younger sisters married his mother's two elder brothers). Raghu's nuclear family, though, sat a full kilometer away. In those years, a kilometer meant a walk. "You can't eat at one place and walk back," he says. That small distance mattered: it separated them from a cousin set that treated school as an obligation, not a pursuit.

Raghu's mother made education non-negotiable. She wasn't formally educated and rarely permitted to decide anything in her own life – raised under a dominant mother, then married into a patriarchal household. But with her children, her will was absolute. Summers, she had them copy the newspaper into notebooks "so we don't lose our handwriting." She borrowed from brothers for tuition when money ran out. She insisted on excellence in a family where "passing was good." And she did it without guarantees – no promise her kids would get better jobs, or take care of her later. "She just did it because it had to be done," Raghu says.

ALWAYS IN THE GAME

At home there was no gender line. Raghu's sister's friends studied at their place; she got the new textbooks, he took her hand-me-downs, and his went to their brother – same with clothes. When she chose the UPSC track and then IPS (not IAS/IFS), the family backed it. "You want to go to Delhi? Go. You want IPS? Do IPS." Raghu says it took him years to understand gender discrimination existed elsewhere.

Money was tight. "There was absolutely no money." Much of their education ran on credit. One year, all three were in engineering at once (his sister in final year, Raghu in third, his brother in first). After Raghu graduated, he joined Texas Instruments – "a paymaster" – and worked two years to help clear debt and support the household until his brother had a job. Only then did he go to IIM Ahmedabad. The MBA dream had started as a kid, cycling past IIM Bangalore en route to Bannerghatta Zoo. Someone told him: study here and you can make ₹50,000 a month. "I was like, ₹50,000 a month?" He had offers from all the IIMs, but he chose the IIMA.

School set early expectations. His sister was the star. So much so that teachers marked attendance with "Radhika's first brother" and "Radhika's second brother." He had always been in her shadow. Then, in Class 10, he scored a state rank – 10th in Karnataka – and his photo appeared in the papers. For the first time, he was visible not just as someone's brother, but in his own right.

In Classes 11-12, the weight of being "the Bangalore topper" pushed him into performance and positioning. "Plus one and plus two went like a flash... I wasn't myself." In engineering, he corrected the course. He topped first year, a senior called him a "loser" for still chasing grades, and he pivoted: organizing fests, raising funds, becoming class rep. He even negotiated away compulsory lab hours – "our hostel computers were better than the lab's" – and became popular for canceling classes and rescheduling assignments.

That period produced a clean leadership moment. In the 2002 recession, Analog Devices came to campus. After its pre-placement talk, they announced they'd hire only one person. Raghu, the CS class rep, stood up before the aptitude test: Computer Science had plenty of IT companies coming; Electronics didn't. "It's better the Electronics guys take this," he said, and walked out. His friends followed. Then the rest of the class. Only later did he recognize what had happened: "I realized I can influence."

The other education was sport. Cricket and football were non-negotiable. "Never in my life was I the twelfth man," he says. "If not captain, I was always on the field." Being "in play" mattered more than outcomes. That ethos extended beyond sport into how he learned from peers. If someone excelled – public speaking, mental math, handwriting – he'd simply ask how. A friend's advice to shed stage fright was blunt: imagine the audience as a bunch of non-judgmental creatures and speak. Raghu tried it, then kept iterating. He maintained multiple circles – Sanskrit-chanting Brahmin friends for antakshari and shlokas, comic-sharing friends from the circulating library, cricket friends, running friends, startup founders. "Very rarely they intersect," he says. The pattern continues today.

Resilience in the family showed up in adult lives too. "Whatever we took up, we never gave up." All three siblings run full marathons; Raghu and his younger brother completed full Ironman races. His sister reversed a mid-career slide in fitness and is now "one of the fittest officers in the country." Raghu insists none of this felt like "resilience" at the time: "It was a way of life... Failure wasn't even discussed."

He describes himself then as short-tempered, with a strong point of view. His mother worried he'd live at the extremes – either do very well or turn antisocial. The same drive could power both outcomes. The family's job was to keep the vector pointed right.

Entrepreneurship wasn't the plan. "There was no entrepreneur bug." The home culture he grew up in was service-oriented, not business-oriented. One of Raghu's IIM batchmates jumped straight to founding; he joined Feedback Ventures in infrastructure consulting. The choice felt logical: India was about to pour money into highways, metros, the Commonwealth Games build-out. He sat for only that company on campus and got in. TaxiForSure would come later.

Underneath, the thread from childhood never changed: he needed to be on the field. He doesn't believe he's special – "If somebody else can do it, I can do it; if I can do it, somebody else can do it" – but he refuses the sidelines. The boy who wouldn't be the twelfth man grew into the founder who, even after a celebrated exit, couldn't accept being done.

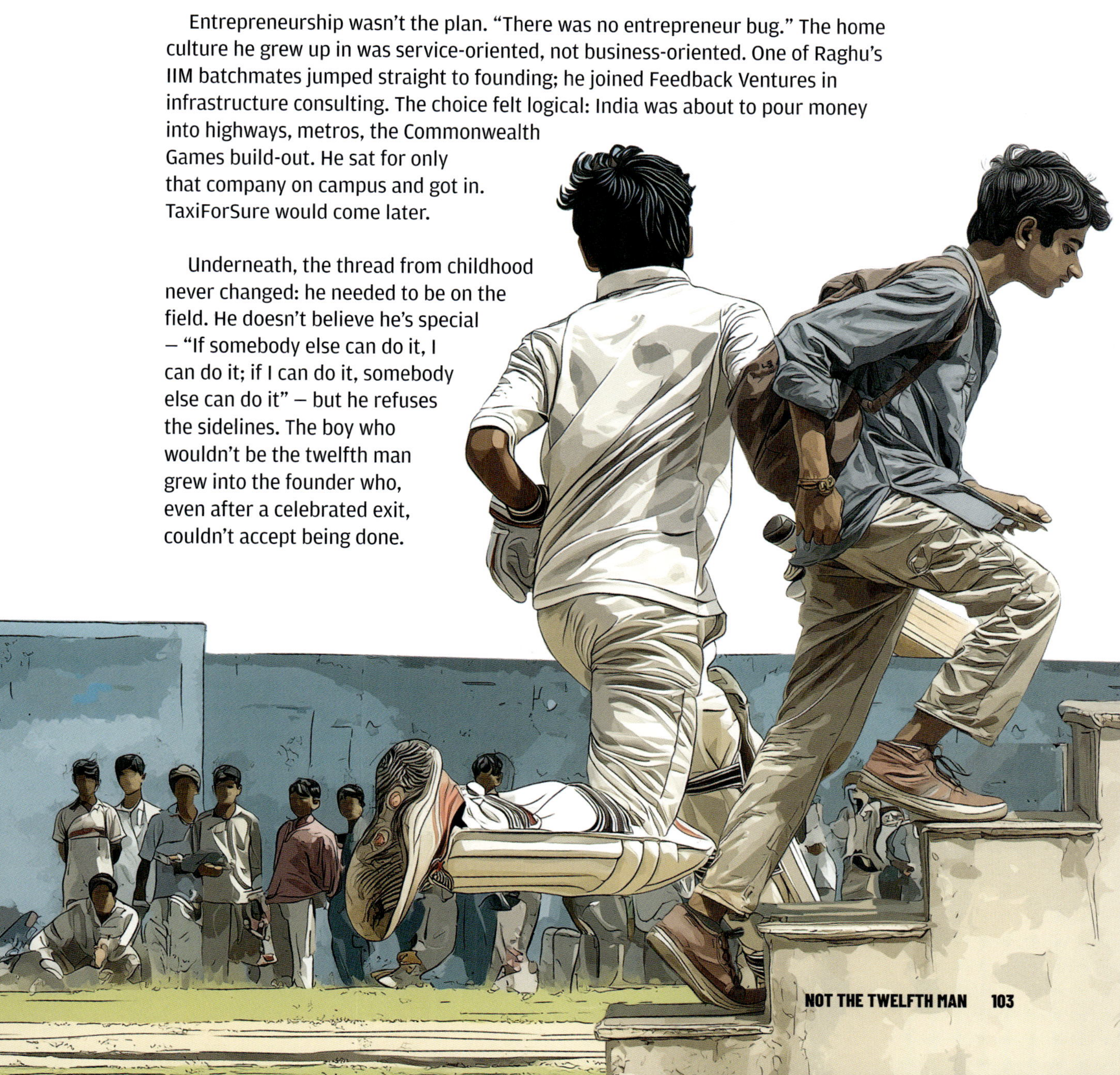

BUILDING SIMPLE, NOT FANCY

The seed of TaxiForSure was scribbled on a tissue at Tavern, a pub on Church Street. Raghu and Aprameya had been grumbling about their jobs and about taxis. Airport drops that cost half a month's salary, cars that sat idle all day, call-center numbers that never picked up. On the napkin they wrote: if you can see empty taxis on the road, why can't you match them to people who need them?

The next morning Raghu found the tissue still in his pocket. They didn't rush to quit. They ran surveys. First with classmates. Then with volunteers outside malls. Of 2,800 people, 92% said they faced the same problem. It was not just B-school kids cribbing. The gap was real. Money was not. Raghu's wife, Shilpa, moved to Singapore, joined DBS, and wired savings back each month. Friends said they couldn't risk it – housing EMIs, marriages. The two of them went ahead alone.

Their office was a single terrace room in JP Nagar, about a hundred square feet, behind the Raghavendra Swamy temple. That room became the company's anchor. In 2015, Raghu would return there to sign the Ola acquisition papers.

The way he described the business was blunt: "People call for a taxi, we send a taxi. It's not complicated." The backbone was a call center. Operators and drivers mattered more than code. Early operations ran on a Google spreadsheet. Only after an investor pointed out how fragile that was did they sit up one night and build a working backend.

The first paying customer was a Yahoo employee who booked a 2 a.m. airport drop from Koramangala. Raghu and Aprameya turned up in person. They checked the cab, wiped down the seats with towels. When the two women passengers came down with their suitcases and saw three men waiting outside in the dark, they panicked. They threw their bags over the compound wall rather than open the gate. Raghu pulled up his LinkedIn profile on his phone to prove who he was. Years later, one of the women recognized him when Raghu told the story at a campus talk.

That was the reality of the early months: a bar napkin, family savings invested from Singapore, a terrace office, a call center, and two founders trying to convince customers they could be trusted.

From a drunken night at a pub to a taxi aggregator startup.

WHEN CAPITAL BECAME A WEAPON

By late 2014, TaxiForSure was steady. Profitable in the cities it chose, enough money in the bank, customers growing. Then on October 28, SoftBank wired $210 million into rival Ola.

The timing, Raghu says, was lethal.

"If that had happened two months before, we'd have been finished. If it had happened two months later, we would have closed $150-250 million and been fine. It was sheer timing."

He answered with numbers. October 31: 6,800 rides. November 14: 16,000. November 21: 22,000. November 30: 31,000. Each week he sent investors a mail – what had been fixed, what still wasn't, what next week would tackle.

"Those mails built a narrative. They went back and read the old ones. They could see the trajectory, not just a single data point. Investors said they had never seen a company move like that."

By early December, multiple funds were calling. Raghu booked twenty-three meetings with investment committees and boarded a flight to the U.S. on December 6 carrying the momentum of November.

That flight split his world. He left India with a growth story. He landed into a ban. The same weekend, an Uber driver in Delhi raped a passenger; by Monday, the government had announced that all taxi apps – Uber, Ola, TaxiForSure – were illegal.

The meetings flipped. Instead of scale, investors wanted to know: would Uber even survive India? Would the model itself survive? Raghu argued back. There was no official notification. Operations hadn't stopped. Demand had spiked with the front-page coverage. He even offered escrow: wire the money, he wouldn't touch it until clarity came. The LPs shook their heads.

"It is very difficult for us to invest $250 million in a company where the government is saying 'banned'."

Back in Delhi, Raghu's co-founder, Aprameya Radhakrishna, was being summoned by police commissioners, forming an improvised industry body with Ola and Uber to argue for survival. Raghu was alone in U.S. boardrooms.

Things changed overnight, and being in a different geography, away from his co-founder and team, did not help.

Later he understood the structural damage: with SoftBank entrenched in Ola, the rest of the pipeline froze.

"If there is no visibility for a Series D, nobody will do a Series C either."

The game itself had degenerated.

"We raised capital only to fight each other – discount customers, incentivize drivers, screw up the entire market. There was zero innovation…"

Capital had become a weapon, not fuel for innovation. One check had rewritten the landscape.

For TaxiForSure, November's surge ended as salvage mode.

We never expected someone would write that check so soon.

WHY OLA, NOT UBER

By February 2015, less than $2 million was left in the bank. Payroll for 1,800 employees loomed, and operators were pressing for clarity. With time, money, and options running out, the runway was effectively gone. The choice was stark: sell or collapse.

One conversation helped Raghu frame the choice. He met Phanindra Sama, founder of redBus, at a Café Coffee Day in Indiranagar. Sama had lived his own exit, selling to Ibibo in 2013, and knew the emotional scars. An employee had once confronted him: “Phani, just like you, we also gave our blood, sweat, and tears. Why is it that you are the only one making money?” Sama had asked what the employee wanted. The answer: “One month’s salary as a bonus will do.”

Sama’s advice was blunt.

“If you’re selling, at least make sure your people feel it mattered. Give them two months’ bonus. Accelerate their ESOPs.”

Raghu absorbed it. That became the red line: no deal without two months’ bonus and ESOP acceleration for TaxiForSure’s team.

The second red line came from Uber itself. Negotiations with them went far. On paper, their offer might have been better. But the model was brutal. Globally, Uber had only 848 employees; TaxiForSure had 1,800 in India. Uber’s driver-only approach meant operators – the fleet owners who anchored TFS’s supply – were redundant. So were most of its people.

“If the deal went through, it would have been a bloodbath. Ninety percent of our people would have had to go.”

For Raghu, that mattered. He refused to hand his company over to an acquirer who would erase the team that built it.

That left Ola. Ola agreed to continue with the operator model and to retain the team.

The price wasn’t what Raghu had once envisioned. But it came with survival for his people.

“We did it for employees, drivers, customers, investors. Failure was never an option. We did it for others.”

In the end, TaxiForSure went to Ola. Not because it was the richest deal, but because it was the only one that preserved dignity for the people inside.

THE TWELFTH MAN YEARS

The sale to Ola closed the TaxiForSure chapter, but it didn't deliver closure. Raghu walked out with reputation intact, money in the bank, and a vacuum inside.

He tried to fill it with a new fintech venture. On paper, it looked right. He built the early team and closed a top-tier bank partnership. But fissures appeared quickly – visions didn't align, and the big picture felt off. A mentor advised stepping back rather than forcing the wrong fit. He exited.

What followed was a three-year stretch where he seemed, from the outside, to be everywhere. He invested in and advised leading Indian startups. He sat in boardrooms, joined founder huddles, and offered lessons from TaxiForSure's scars.

Inside, it gnawed at him.

"I became the twelfth man," he says. "You still get a medal if the team wins. But you don't get to play."

The line captures the paradox. He was visible, even celebrated, but absent from the field. For someone who had grown up insisting he would never sit out, the role of advisor and investor felt like exile.

He tried to channel the void into physical extremes. In 2015, he registered for an Ironman triathlon before even knowing how to swim. He learned in pools, then in open water, then in ocean currents. In 2017, he completed a full Ironman. His sister and younger brother – both marathoners – joined the pursuit. "Whatever we took up, we never gave up."

The finish lines didn't resolve the restlessness. They only proved endurance. The hunger that had driven TaxiForSure was still there, unspent.

The lesson of those years was sharp: reputation, investments, medals – they were substitutes. What he really wanted was to be back on the pitch.

By 2018, Raghu had tried almost everything except the one thing that mattered: building again. Even the Ironman medals, hard-earned as they were, couldn't change the truth.

The hunger to be back on the pitch was unresolved. He wanted a problem that demanded his full presence, the way TaxiForSure once had.

That's where 2019 brought a spark.

VALID HERE, INVALID THERE

By 2019, Raghu's years on the sidelines had hardened into restlessness. The investor meetings, the twelfth-man metaphor, even the Ironman finish lines hadn't closed the loop. What he wanted was a problem that demanded his full presence.

The spark came far from India. Over dinner in the U.S., a friend – an engineer with a secure job – pulled out cash to settle the bill. No card.

It jarred him.

"Your engineering degree is valid here. But your credit history is not?"

Once seen, the contradiction stayed. Skilled migrants could cross borders, join the best companies, earn top salaries – and still be invisible to financial systems.

He began to notice it everywhere. A group of Portuguese founders in the Valley, living cash-first lives. An Israeli ex-founder at Google, drawing $1.2 million a year, yet offered only a $250 credit card. His own mentor, Subrata Mitra, turned down for an Amex after returning to India.

This wasn't an Indian problem, or an American problem. It was systemic. Banks and regulators still assumed a lifetime in one country, one credit file. Cross a border and your history vanished. The result: whole communities of engineers, students, and entrepreneurs living as if on probation, despite strong incomes.

For Raghu, it was the inverse of TaxiForSure. There, he had burned money to prove a need. Here, the need was already written into millions of daily lives.

The recognition gave him what the twelfth-man years had denied: a field to step onto. This was not a thought experiment or a board seat. It was a lived gap, urgent and global. The insight was simple to state, impossible to ignore: creditworthiness should travel with you.

The harder part – and the part he was finally ready for – was turning that clarity into a structure that could not be knocked over.

A problem he couldn't unsee.

BUILDING ZOLVE DIFFERENTLY

Raghu wanted Zolve to carry its scars in the open. His previous startup, TaxiForSure had taught him what it meant to be outgunned by capital, pulled into side bets, and slowed by teams learning on the job. This time, he wanted the structure itself to tilt the game.

The first choice was investors. At TFS, rival Ola's over $200 million raise from SoftBank froze every funding conversation. At Zolve, he handpicked backers whose names and balance sheets would make the category non-contestable.

The second decision was focus. TaxiForSure had shown Raghu where his strengths lay. "I realized I was better at building B2C businesses," he says. Knowing this, he deliberately backed B2C startups as an investor in the years after TFS. With cross-border fintech, there was an opportunity to go B2B, but he chose not to. Zolve would stay pure B2C. If he engaged in B2B at all, it would be only through small personal angel bets outside the company. The company itself would not drift. The customer was the north star.

The third was team. TFS had been built bottom-up with rookies. At Zolve, he hired laterals – operators who had already navigated compliance, banking partnerships, and cross-border execution. It meant slower hiring, but fewer fatal errors.

The fourth was credibility at the gate. Fintechs lived and died by how regulators and partners perceived them. By bringing HSBC in as a minority investor, he prepaid that credibility. "HSBC-funded" opened doors everywhere.

Each choice inverted an earlier wound. The taxi wars showed what unchecked burn could do. A past fintech stint showed how valuation games corrode teams. The advisory years showed how brittle compliance could snap companies overnight.

Zolve wasn't designed to be another startup. It was designed so that when the next shock came, it would still stand.

THE NEW PHILOSOPHY

The years between TaxiForSure and Zolve stripped Raghu of illusions. He stopped believing in "open markets." The taxi wars had shown him that capital, not efficiency, decides outcomes and that unchecked, it can wreck industries and leave founders hollow.

His view of entrepreneurship shifted. It was no longer about catching waves or timing luck. It was about design over drift. Choose investors who close the category, not ones who keep doors ajar. Build credibility into the structure at the start, not as a scramble later. Hire operators who already carry scars, not rookies you must train mid-battle. Each was a correction drawn from wounds: the burn of 2014 and the fragility he saw while advising others.

And beneath all of it was something older. The teenager who refused to be the twelfth man in cricket. The founder who, even after a $200 million exit in 2015, could not accept that his story was finished.

"Entrepreneurship is unfinished by design. It's not about closure. It's about self-discovery. I want to play. Even if I lose."

That is what endures. Not multiples, not headlines, not applause. The point is to stay on the field.

06

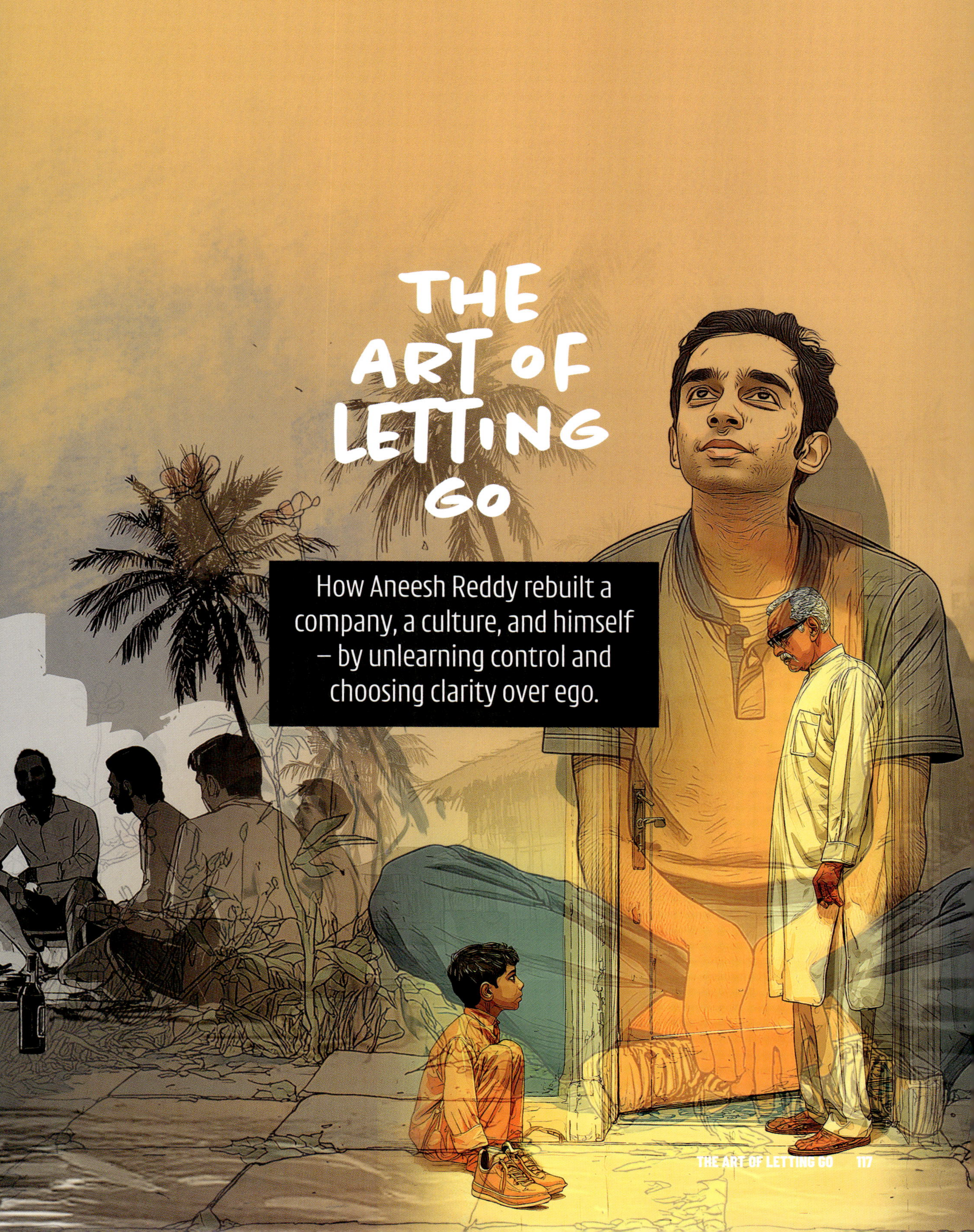

THE ART OF LETTING GO

How Aneesh Reddy rebuilt a company, a culture, and himself – by unlearning control and choosing clarity over ego.

LIFE HAS A PLAN

Aneesh Reddy didn't realize it that night in Goa, sitting by a small bonfire with the same friends he'd had since nursery, that he was doing something he hadn't done in eleven years. He was pausing.

On paper, nothing was on fire. Capillary was steady, the kind of steady he had craved for years. But while the others laughed and looped old jokes, his drink stayed untouched. His heel kept pressing into the sand, as if to make sure he was really there.

When the lull came, he heard himself say it:

"I think from here...life only goes downhill."

It was the first time he could hear the static he'd been living inside – the constant fixing, chasing, proving – and not rush to drown it out. For once, he didn't fill the silence. He let the sentence sit in the ocean breeze. Karthik, his friend, just looked at him. He didn't try to fix it. That helped.

That pause had an older root, in a very different heat.

When Aneesh was two, his parents sent him back from Iran to Hyderabad so they could keep working as doctors abroad to clear family debt and build a base for the family. He grew up moving every couple of years between aunts' homes – three kitchens, three sets of rules, three rhythms. He learned to adapt without complaint. He didn't control the house; he learned its patterns and found his place in them.

By the time his parents returned, he thought he understood how to keep his footing anywhere. And then came Kharagpur.

He had wanted IIT Madras. His JEE rank – 1342 – sent him to Kharagpur instead. It felt like a sentence, not a plan. The first evening, he hung his only neatly pressed white shirt on a hook, lifted it an hour later, and watched white choona from the wall stain the shoulder. The bathroom light flickered. A lizard sat by the switch, and he stood outside with a towel, negotiating with a reptile. Mess food was mostly rice. The dust didn't care for creases.

By mid-year, he had dropped from eighty-five kilos to fifty-eight. His mother thought it was TB. He didn't have a name for it – just the knowledge that he wasn't in control. One day in the library, he underlined a line from Sri Aurobindo: "Pain is the hammer of God." He didn't understand it, but he closed the book gently.

The shift came without announcement. One blackout night, Krishna Mehra – known as KK – and Aneesh lay on their bunks, mosquitoes whining. KK said, "We'll probably miss this someday." Aneesh laughed – properly. The light didn't have to come back for the moment to be okay.

It took that night in Goa to name it: life has a plan.

You don't see it when you're bargaining with a lizard, when your rank re-routes your story, or when your own sentence hangs over a small fire with your oldest friends. But if you loosen your hold for a minute and look back, there's a pattern. The places Aneesh didn't choose – Kharagpur, the factory floor, the rooms where co-founders said they were done – taught him more than the ones he tried to engineer.

Kharagpur was the first time he stopped believing inputs guarantee outcomes. Goa was the first time he caught himself living like that might be true. That night, letting go stopped feeling like collapse. It started feeling like a choice.

MANY HOMES, ONE RHYTHM

Aneesh Reddy didn't learn adaptability from books. He learned it by changing pillows.

Every couple of years, his bed and the rules around it changed. He wasn't visiting relatives; he was living in their houses. He watched for cues: the first tea whistle, the first voice in the corridor, the things that meant it was his turn.

At Nanni Aunty's 1BHK, belonging felt like a matinee. Movie tickets were tucked under a plastic bowl of popcorn, the pedestal fan rattling at full speed, cousins sprawled on the floor. Space was short; warmth wasn't. If you showed up, you belonged.

At Pedramakka's, belonging had a clock. Milk at six sharp, beds folded by 6:10, no second call – "Aneesh! Aditya!" from the corridor was both invitation and deadline. She was called a "terror," but nothing was arbitrary. Keep rhythm, earn ease.

At Buji's, belonging shared bandwidth with four kids and a kitchen always in motion. In two years, they watched one movie together. That wasn't neglect; it was arithmetic. Someone always had a test, a fever, or a turn at the sink. Aneesh learned to pick his battles and be okay when it wasn't his turn.

Threading through all of this was his grandfather, Krishna Reddy – bath, prayer, work, every day, no exceptions. He sent Aneesh's mother into medicine and was ready to pay a donation if she hadn't earned her seat outright. He didn't preach values. He lived them. The house moved to his clock.

Hyderabad loved comparisons. Aneesh's older brother, Aditya, was a state topper. Aneesh wasn't bitter. He calibrated differently. If Aditya brought home trophies, Aneesh lined up the shoes, pressed the sleeves, kept the place running. The adults noticed. That taught him that steadiness could be its own currency.

If there was one thread from those years, it was this: belonging was a skill. He learned to read rooms quickly – where warmth got him in, where rigor did, where silence did. And another: he could switch codes without losing himself.

That muscle explained choices that baffled people later. When he turned down MIT and signed ITC at 8:03 a.m., it wasn't rebellion against prestige; it was the muscle memory of choosing fit over shine. The lab gave him papers; the E-Cell and robotics club gave him life.

It explained the ITC factory floor too. When older workers in Bangalore crossed their arms and told him in Kannada to speak their language if he wanted to lead, he recognized the ask. It wasn't policy they wanted. It was to be seen on their terms.

And it shaped Capillary's early operating style. At KK's family's old building in Girish Park, they shipped at the client's tempo. Later, they made it policy: budgets opened quarterly, not annually; they hired for fit before flash. Could someone solve five live problems, with these people, at this cadence? If yes, welcome. If no, no hard feelings.

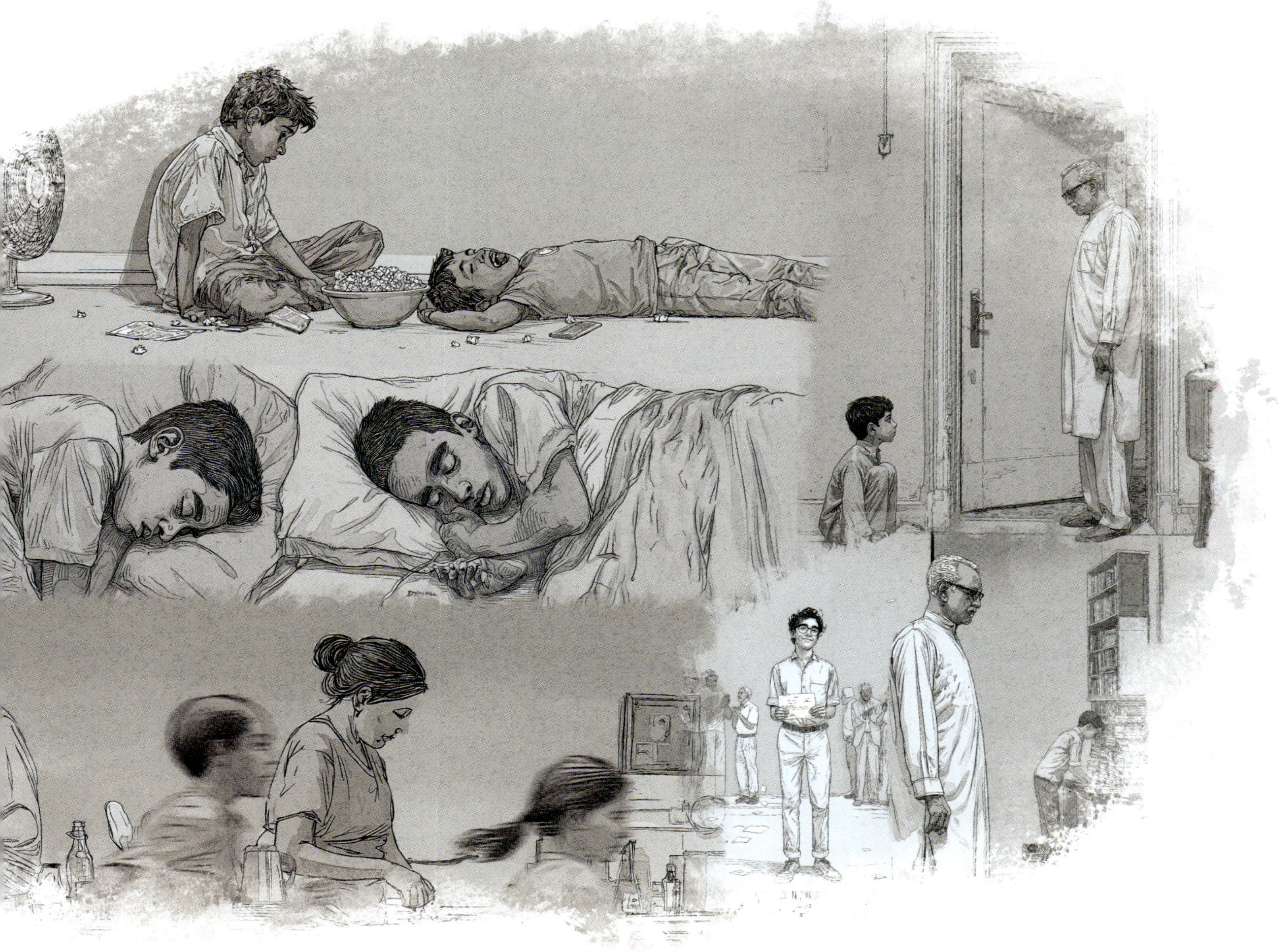

The Plan You Didn't Make

Pain is the hammer of God

THE GIRISH PARK TEMPO

Girish Park wasn't a "garage startup." It was KK's family's old building in North Kolkata – cracked marble on the stairs, air that smelled faintly of damp cloth, paint older than them peeling into soft curls. The ceiling fan clattered more than it cooled. Their first table was borrowed, the second chair didn't match, and the Wi-Fi came from an unsecured network they didn't ask too many questions about.

They had ₹15 lakh from IIT Kharagpur's incubation cell – the same program Aneesh and KK had fought for years earlier as students, convincing the campus to fund ventures in exchange for small equity. That check didn't feel like capital. It felt like permission – permission to try, to break something on Monday and fix it on Tuesday.

They didn't start with a big idea. They started with a shared frustration:

KK: "Nothing I build ever ships."

Aneesh: "I don't even know if my work matters."

That was enough. The year was 2008.

Their first client, Indus League, looked at their proposal, slid the server box back across the desk, and said, "We don't want hardware. Just charge us monthly." They had never heard of Salesforce. They didn't know "SaaS" was a category. They wrote "₹2,000/store/month" on a whiteboard and moved on.

A month later, Lehman Brothers collapsed. Retail froze. Half the market they thought they were building for disappeared. But the grant money was still in the bank, and they still had the room. So they stayed. Shipped what they could. Called whoever would take the call.

That room taught them more than frugality. It taught tempo. Code should move at the speed of a customer conversation. Invoices should move at the speed of trust. Nothing stayed on the backlog if the customer wouldn't use it in the next quarter.

The habit stuck. In 2009, when Qualcomm's QPrize money came in – $100,000 that kept them alive – they didn't change pace. They were still wiring fixes to stores at 2 a.m., still treating every renewal like the first sale.

Years later, when they over-hired, got burned in China, or found that MartJack's numbers didn't match reality, the only recoveries that worked were when they went back to Girish Park mode: something small, useful, this week, for a customer whose name they knew.

Girish Park set the company's rhythm. Not because it was romantic, but because there was no space for drama. They either shipped or they didn't. The customer either used it or they didn't. Once Aneesh had worked with that kind of honesty, it was hard to build any other way.

SIX NEAR-DEATHS

Aneesh Reddy used to think survival came from force – more hours, more calls, more will. Then he lived through the same movie six times. The opening scenes changed; the middle and ending never did.

1 – August 2009: The grant runs dry

The ₹10 lakh he and KK had convinced IIT Kharagpur's incubation cell to give them was gone. Aneesh went back to the same office they had helped set up, not to boast but to ask for more. Another ₹5 lakh bought them months, not certainty. That was the first time he learned you didn't have to win to survive. You just had to buy time without panicking.

2 – November 2009: Angels late, plastic maxed

Aneesh and KK hadn't drawn salaries for eighteen months. Credit cards were maxed. At 2 a.m., Aneesh sat refreshing a bank page that didn't change. Then Qualcomm's QPrize came in – $100,000 and a headline that made other checks easier to ask for. That night, he stopped believing survival was about genius. It was about oxygen and timing.

3 – Mid-2011: The pivot we didn't do

An investor promised money if they became a consumer company. They stalled for months, even hired ahead of the decision. Then they said no. The term sheet vanished. Payroll turned into a calendar with red circles around Thursdays. Qualcomm and a few early angels stepped in again – not because the deck dazzled, but because they had kept their promises and their books clean. Credibility became a survival currency.

4 – 2012: The Singapore flip limbo

They redomiciled to attract global capital. The money got stuck in paperwork no one could speed up. At home, the balance wheezed. One incoming investor wired a bridge just hours before salaries were due and rent bounced. At the time, it felt heroic. Later, Aneesh filed it under the same heading as every other save: luck.

5 – 2014: The fracture and the runway

KK was out. Ajay was done. An investor who had promised a bridge pulled it the day the board chose Aneesh to lead alone. He wrote "forty-five days" at the top of the whiteboard and stared at it like it was a countdown clock. People he thought would be there forever handed in resignations without a tremor. Weeks later, the same investor came back; Asia had tripled; a new round closed. They didn't survive because of heroics. They survived because the one part of the business they hadn't neglected was still compounding quietly.

6 – April 2020: Covid drops the floor

Revenue was down 80%. They cut, but with dignity as the measure. Two hundred people left, and every one was placed. Two weeks later, a $5 million bridge landed – not because they looked invincible, but because investors could smell stewardship that was real.

Across these six, the pattern wasn't heroics. It was bluntness: money came late, wires failed, somebody blinked, and pride didn't pay bills. The only reasons Capillary was still standing were small promises kept, a product people actually used, friends who answered calls at midnight, and luck that refused to leave entirely.

Aneesh has said this out loud because it needs to be said: luck is 90% of entrepreneurship. Everyone works hard. Everyone bleeds. The ones who don't make it are not less capable. They just run out of oxygen before the weather clears.

Those years took something from him – the belief that inputs guarantee outcomes. What they gave back was quieter and, he learned, more durable: equanimity. By the sixth storm, he didn't feel triumphant. He felt tired and honest. The next time survival was on the line – in the 2019 burn, in the November '22 knife-edge – he didn't reach for more grip. He asked the only questions that mattered: What can I control? Who should I call? What can I let go?

That was the real gift of living through near-death six times. Not swagger. Pattern recognition.

THE COST OF AMBITION

When Warburg's $45 million hit Capillary's account in 2015, it felt to Aneesh Reddy as if they had been handed a new set of tools for the same job. He told himself more capital would mean more discipline, more reach, more credibility. He should have remembered what Girish Park had taught them – rhythm matters more than size.

The first "more" was MartJack. On paper, it was perfect: an e-commerce platform with steady revenue, exactly what their retail clients needed to go omnichannel. In reality, they closed too fast and looked too little. Revenues were inflated, churn was hidden, invoicing was sloppy. Within months, they had to write off nearly a third of its topline. What Aneesh thought would be a growth engine became a drain – on focus, morale, and trust.

The second "more" was China and the SME mid-market. They told themselves churn was a fixable problem if they moved faster than the competition. They told themselves China's size would outweigh its price wars and regulatory landmines. Both bets bled cash. Both pulled leadership attention away from the enterprise loyalty core they actually knew how to win.

And then came the sales-and-marketing balloon. In less than a year, their global S&M headcount went from about fifteen to nearly a hundred. Veterans from big companies brought polish – and politics. Order books fattened, but renewals slipped. Collaboration frayed. People who had built Capillary in the lean years – some for over a decade – began walking out. Seeing them resign was worse than the MartJack write-off; it was proof that the culture they had assumed was permanent could, in fact, be lost.

By early 2019, the math was brutal: $2 million a month in burn, growth stalled, morale thin. In a boardroom that had once been Aneesh's arena, he laid out numbers he couldn't spin. This wasn't a market collapse or a co-founder walk-out. It was self-inflicted – his appetite for "more" had outpaced their systems, their cash discipline, and his own ability to see what was right in front of him.

The fix was unglamorous. In five quarters, Capillary went from a 60% EBITDA loss to breakeven. Anant stepped in as COO/CFO, tearing through every cost line like a customs officer looking for contraband. Sridhar merged their regional delivery org into one global team, killing redundancies they had let fester. Piyush and Pravanjan went deep on product automation, easing the pressure on the front-end scramble. Aneesh did his own cutting – not just budgets, but pet bets he had once sold to the board as "strategic."

They got back to profitability. But the lesson stayed like a splinter: unchecked ambition doesn't just burn cash – it burns trust, clarity, and the muscle memory that got them there in the first place.

By the end of 2019, they were smaller, saner, and finally cash-positive. On paper, that looked like a turnaround. In Aneesh's head, it felt like a confession: they had had to relearn how to run a business without lying to themselves about what "more" would cost.

THE FRACTURE WAS HIM

KK wasn't just a co-founder. He was two doors down from Aneesh in Kharagpur – the guy who stayed up through power cuts talking about what they'd build "once they got out." By the time they started Capillary, Aneesh didn't call him a friend. He called him family.

Six years later, that family was split across three time zones: KK in California, Ajay in Bangalore, Aneesh in Singapore. They still worked in the same Google Docs, but their conversations lived in the margins – short comments, occasional jabs – and when they spoke, it was usually to disagree.

The argument by 2014 was the U.S. business. KK wanted more engineering firepower; Aneesh wanted to keep the bulk in Asia, where the unit economics made sense. They stopped listening, started defending positions like territory.

At a board meeting in Singapore, KK walked out before Aneesh did. Neither of them turned. He had said it before, but that day it stuck: "You've become a bully." Not a jab. A mirror. And Aneesh didn't argue.

Weeks later, Ajay and Aneesh took a morning walk around their apartment complex – cold air, empty swings, the kind of quiet that makes the next sentence heavy. Ajay didn't waste words. "I'm tired, Aneesh." By the end of the month, he was gone too.

Forty-five days of cash. A whiteboard split in two columns – moved on and still here – with names Aneesh had thought would never leave now on the first side. This wasn't a market collapse or a product miss. This was him. And that was the hardest diagnosis: the kind you can't outwork.

Venkat, one of the board members, told Aneesh to get a coach. He expected frameworks and pep talks. Instead, the first session ended with a spiral-bound 360° report – twenty people's anonymous feedback boiled down to a single line that hit harder than any funding rejection: "He doesn't realize how intimidating he is."

He read it and stayed still. No explanations. No "but you don't understand." Just the slow recognition that this was how he'd been showing up, even when he thought he was helping.

The old reflex would have been to fix it himself, to prove them wrong with longer hours. But you can't outwork a trust fracture. You can't spreadsheet your way back into someone's confidence. Trust is rebuilt in the space you give, not the control you grip.

For months, Aneesh didn't defend himself to anyone. He sat with the silence, the smaller attendance in meetings, the realization that culture had been shifting under his feet without him noticing. It was the same helplessness he had felt his first week in Kharagpur, staring at a wall that didn't care about his pressed shirt. Only this time, it wasn't the wall. It was him.

That year broke something — in a good way. The arrogance, the belief that willpower alone could carry any weight, the need to force outcomes. Painful as it was, it cleared space for something he didn't know he'd need later: the possibility that he didn't have to have all the answers.

"KK walked out, Ajay said he was tired, the whiteboard showed forty-five days of cash. Then came the 360° report: He doesn't realize how intimidating he is."

STRENGTH IN ASKING

For most of his career, Aneesh Reddy thought strength meant carrying it all. If a wire was late, he would find a bridge. If a quarter slipped, he would outwork the slip. Pride didn't strut – it sat quietly in the reflex to solve alone.

November 2022 cracked that reflex.

Two days before payroll, the debt deal they had been counting on went cold. One short message: "Not wiring." Aneesh opened the bank page – ₹1.8 crore in the account. Just below that were the bills that kept them alive: AWS at ₹1.7 crore, Airtel at ₹1.3 crore. You could delay a hire. You couldn't delay the platforms the customers ran on, or the salaries that kept their families fed.

The old Aneesh would have shut the door, worked the phones until midnight, and patched the gap in secret. This time, Vipassana was still in his bones. He sat, watched the panic rise, and didn't wrestle with it. This will also pass. That didn't make him passive. It made him exact: What now?

The answer was uncomfortable – call his family.

He started with his father. He had never asked him for money. Not once. His parents had spent his first years in Iran as doctors, clearing debts and saving for the family. They had sent him back to Hyderabad before he turned two, trusting his aunts and grandfather to raise him. Asking wasn't in his wiring.

"Dad," he said, "we're in a tough spot. I need your help."

No hesitation. No lecture. Just: "Of course, Aneesh. Whatever you need."

Next was Mammaya – his father-in-law. A seasoned entrepreneur, he didn't let Aneesh finish before saying yes. Calm. Immediate. No drama.

And then came the call Aneesh hadn't expected to make. Years earlier, two former Capillary teammates had started Gameberry Labs. He had been there for them in their early, messy days – not with checks, but with time, advice, quiet backing. That week, before he had finished explaining, they wired the money. "You've been there for us. We've got you."

They made payroll. They kept the lights on. But what stayed with Aneesh wasn't the rescue – it was the crack in his old story about strength. He had told himself for years that asking was weakness, that founders lone-wolfed their way through. The truth was plainer: most things hold better when you let people in.

It didn't end with the crisis. He stopped performing certainty for the board. He opened the numbers wider inside the company. He asked leaders to carry their share with him – not for him.

Acceptance didn't make him softer. It made him specific. Sometimes what now was a spreadsheet. Sometimes it was a phone call that loosened a muscle he had had clenched for twenty years.

He used to think the work was carrying everything. Now he knew the work was knowing what was his to carry – and who to call when it wasn't.

DESIGNING FOR PEACE

By April 2020, Aneesh Reddy had lived through enough knife-edges to know that gripping harder wasn't the answer. Covid shut the world down and took 80% of Capillary's revenue with it. Twenty days of cash.

The younger Aneesh would have defaulted to overdrive – raise at any cost, push the team to exhaustion, hold every thread himself. Vipassana had stripped that reflex out. The job now was to decide, cleanly, what to hold and what to let go.

They cut, but the metric wasn't survival. It was dignity. Two hundred people left during those months, and every single one was placed. The leadership team turned into an outplacement crew – mapping networks, calling peers, opening doors in other companies. Aneesh's line on every Zoom stayed the same: "They gave us years. Let's give them a soft landing." It wasn't optics; it was the only measure that mattered.

The same posture held in early 2023 when the IPO window, months in the making, slammed shut after a market rout. The younger Aneesh would have forced it, gambling on market forgiveness. This time, he closed the laptop. Not the moment. That was okay. It wasn't surrender. It was design.

That design came from stripping the work to what they could actually control. Budgets opened quarterly, not annually. They told the board what was real, not what looked good on a slide. They hadn't missed EBITDA in three years, even when top-line targets slipped.

Aneesh ran his own life the same way, with a two-by-two: health, spirituality, friends and family, and Capillary. If one box stayed empty for too long, something changed. It was how he caught himself before the old patterns crept in – before he said yes to the eleventh meeting, before email swallowed meditation, before growth experiments crowded out the core.

From the outside, it looked like subtraction – fewer distractions, fewer bets, shutting down what didn't serve the core. Inside, it was the opposite. It was endurance. You stopped living on adrenaline and started living on rhythm.

Operational peace wasn't retreat. It was an engineering problem: build the floor strong enough, the pillars sound enough, so the roof stood without you propping it up. Only then could you step back and know it would hold.

HE DOESN'T REALIZE
HOW INTIMIDATING HE IS.

CARRYING IT BACK

Aneesh Reddy went to Pocharam, a Vipassana meditation center on the outskirts of Hyderabad, in February 2020 because a friend told him he needed a reset. Ten days of silence sounded extreme, even self-indulgent. He didn't expect that the hardest part wouldn't be the silence. It would be carrying it back.

Since then, every morning for him has started on the cushion. Forty-five minutes. The same instruction: notice the breath, notice the body, don't push, don't pull. Some days it's calm; some days his head is a spreadsheet. But he sits. That's the point. You don't get to skip because it's noisy inside.

The discipline isn't exotic. It's the same muscle his grandfather had modelled: bath, prayer, work – every day, no exceptions. Vipassana just switched the medium from activity to stillness. It didn't make him serene. It made him precise about where his attention goes, and where it has no business going.

He and his team built that precision into Capillary's culture. Leaders now get Vipassana leave – not as a perk, but as preparation. If someone is making calls that affect hundreds of people, they should know what their mind does when the inputs stop. The ones who've taken it return different: more patient in meetings, slower to interrupt, quicker to own mistakes without defensiveness. That changes the texture of the whole room.

You can feel it in the small things. Quarterly reviews with more listening than talking. Debates that pause instead of escalating. Even in hiring – someone who can sit with silence is less likely to panic when the numbers wobble. It's not inefficiency; it's the space where better decisions happen.

The retreat lasts ten days. The sit stays. It's what let Aneesh close the IPO file without drama, pick up the phone in November 2022 without shame, and shut down MartJack before it bled the company further. Those weren't "big" Vipassana moments. They were just decisions made by someone who had practiced not reacting for forty-five minutes every morning.

He doesn't evangelize it. Most people won't do it for ten days. But everyone can take a sit – five minutes before a board call, one breath before answering, a pause before sending that email. Once you've seen how much stronger things hold when you build that space in, it's hard to go back to gripping everything all the time.

LETTING GO AS STRENGTH

For years, Aneesh Reddy thought his job as a founder was to hold everything – the numbers, the decisions, the relationships, the crises. If something broke, he stepped in. If someone left, he filled the gap. If the money ran out, he found a patch. That instinct kept Capillary alive for over a decade. But it almost broke him.

The turning points in his journey weren't the celebrated milestones. They were the moments he had to loosen his hold – watching KK walk out of a boardroom without looking back, calling his father and Mammaya in November 2022 when payroll was days away and the bank balance didn't cover it, shutting down MartJack after months of trying to will it into working.

Each time, pride told him to push through. Ego told him to keep the performance going. But the reality was simple: the company – and he – did better when he stopped pretending he could engineer every outcome.

Letting go wasn't walking away. It was deciding exactly what was his to carry and building the people, systems, and culture that could hold the rest without him in the room. That's why leaders at Capillary now get Vipassana leave – not as a perk, but as maintenance for clarity.

It was the same muscle Aneesh had first built as a child moving between aunts' homes – reading the room, trusting the rhythm, knowing when to adapt. The same muscle he strengthened in Kharagpur, learning that inputs don't guarantee outcomes. The same one he had honed since Vipassana at Pocharam, on the cushion every morning, noticing when his grip tightened and choosing, deliberately, to ease it.

He still steps in when it matters – a key hire, a deal that shapes the next decade. But he doesn't fill the air just to feel in control. Most things hold if you've built them right.

That's the real strength: not in proving you can carry it all, but in knowing what not to carry – and trusting the rest to stand without your hand on it.

07

NOT A UNICORN

Two founders, one fight: Sharat Potharaju and Ravi Pratap Maddimsetty (RPM) on failure and pivots

THE FIRST CLIFF

It is late in Bangalore, the kind of night that feels still but not quiet inside your head. Sharat is on his back, eyes open. This, he says, is his "expertise": "I wake up in the morning and think about worst-case scenarios."

He learned long ago – and keeps relearning – that mapping the disaster first, then working backward, is how he feels prepared. He likes to tell the story of a scene from the movie *Munich*, where the team goes around the table naming their skills and the oldest man says, 'I worry.' Sharat recognizes himself in that role.

The inventory tonight is familiar: forty-plus salaries to meet, a product that no longer belongs to its market, the bank balance now measured in months not years. There is also the middle-class reflex he once described as the "third rat" in a Bulgarian banker's parable – the one that keeps pressing the lever without knowing when, or if, food will drop. Beside him, in the half-dark, Sowmya is asleep, pregnancy just visible. She is the unspoken anchor in the room, the point around which his loop of scenarios and recalculations eventually slow.

Three continents away, in a small U.S. office, Ravi Pratap Maddimsetty, popularly known among peers as RPM, held the operations through the night. The company's U.S. support number doesn't ring at a call center – "it rings on my desk," he says. On his monitor, the support ticket window is open. If a publisher complains about a half-blank page on an older Android device, he wants to hear the steps directly from the voice that's stuck.

If a demo fails mid-meeting, he wants the error reproduced in front of him, not softened into a second-hand report. He has lived this principle for years: founders should hear the pain unfiltered. Later, engineers will rotate through support by design, but here the loop is just him: listen, replicate, fix, ship.

The two scenes – Sharat's insomnia in Bangalore, Ravi's ticket queue in New York – look like opposites until you see the premise they share. One is mapping the cliff's edge so nobody steps off it by accident; the other is testing the ground, one careful step at a time, so it holds. Neither outsources responsibility when outcomes matter.

At home, the soundtrack is domestic: Sowmya's breathing; in Ravi's case, children who will one day imitate his greeting – "Beaconstac support, this is Ravi" – the way they hear it a dozen times a day.

What keeps both lines moving isn't bravado. It's the unromantic discipline of staying close to what's real: the bank balance, the actual error that threw, the person on the other end of the call. Most such nights end not with a breakthrough, but with a simple decision: keep pressing forward.

2015. Two clocks, one question: Is this how it ends?

DELAYED GRATIFICATION

Sharat describes himself, even as a boy, as "the seventh or eighth rank guy every year." Never first, never bottom – just reliably there. In his telling, this wasn't mediocrity, it was identity: the proof that he could hold a line. In Hyderabad's tight academic ladders, consistency was currency. You didn't always win, but you didn't fall out of the race either.

Tennis was his first apprenticeship in politics. On cracked school courts, selection wasn't always about who was best on the day – it was whose parents had tea with the coach. "It taught me merit doesn't guarantee selection," he says. The lesson wasn't cynicism; it was a kind of realism he would see again in business: you can do the work, hit the shots, and still not get the call.

When IIT prep began, the hours were carved out of the rest of his life. He took multiple buses to reach his coaching center, waking at four in the morning, the day mapped to the minute. There were no movies, no dating, no free Saturdays. "Either you made it on the last boat or you didn't." Hyderabad was, and still is, one of the epicenters of that competitive migration. For middle-class families, IIT was more than an exam – it was an escape route, a stamp that unlocked careers and countries.

One image stays with him from those years, brought into his vocabulary years later by a Bulgarian banker mentor. The man had told him there were three kinds of rats: the first presses the lever and the food comes immediately; the second presses and nothing comes, so it stops; the third keeps pressing, not knowing when, or if, the food will drop. "Middle-class life," Sharat says, "is that third rat." The habit of persistence without certainty – and the anxiety it breeds – was something he carried into his company years later, in good markets and bad.

Alongside that pragmatism was a quieter current of ambition shaped by what he read. On his father's insistence, he began reading *The Economist* in his teens – barely understanding 20% of it, but always turning to the obituary section. The people there weren't always famous. They were people who had built institutions that outlived them. Dr Verghese Kurien, the engineer of India's White Revolution, became a touchstone: proof that a single person could change the economics of millions of lives. That mix – of measured persistence, the acceptance that merit isn't always rewarded, and the hunger to build something that would outlast him – was in place long before he wrote a pitch deck.

ORIGINS OF A PARTNERSHIP

They grew up in the same city, Hyderabad, but in different orbits. Sharat was the banker's son, tennis rackets and early mornings on cracked school courts, learning to temper his temper after bad calls without ever pretending the calls were fair. Ravi was the transplant from Delhi, head bent over a second-hand programming manual in a neighborhood computer center, where an older mentor named Bhaskar made him follow one rule: "Don't just copy the code – change something and see what breaks."

Their lessons ran in parallel. Sharat learned that merit didn't guarantee selection, in sport or elsewhere. Ravi learned that competence came in increments, not in flashes of brilliance. By the time Ravi had ground his way from "needs improvement" in mathematics to clearing the IIT-JEE, the habit was embedded: progress was earned draft by draft.

They didn't meet until they were both far from Hyderabad. In 2004, Ravi was a year into his job at Morgan Stanley in New York; Sharat had arrived from Duke to interview on Wall Street. Hotels were out of reach, so he crashed at Ravi's rent-controlled apartment – two single beds, a view of the Hudson filtered through winter haze. The arrangement, meant to last days, extended into months after Sharat joined Merrill Lynch.

Evenings in that small flat became a postgraduate course of their own making. Ravi explained how products were built, how architecture decisions shaped what got shipped, how iteration worked in the open-source world he'd been part of since his Ximian days. Sharat unpacked capital markets – how deals were put together, how clients could be steered or lost. They didn't argue over lanes. Ravi would build; Sharat would sell. That was the unspoken pact.

One night, Ravi wrote a one-pager for a vernacular mobile device built from the ground up for India. Sharat admired the scale of the vision but steered the conversation toward something they could start without hardware. The pragmatism wasn't cynicism; it was the instinct to find an opening they could afford to run at.

By the time either of them put their names on a company registration, the rhythms were already set. They had lived together, worked separately, and learned exactly how the other thought under pressure. Years later, Ravi would say, "We didn't have to discuss whether we could work together – we already knew exactly how we would."

BACKERS WITH A VOTE OF CONFIDENCE

When they finally decided to give up their U.S. jobs and start a company in India in 2009, there was no pitch deck, no demo, no institutional investor waiting to wire money. The only place to go for capital was the people who already knew them.

Sharat began with the network he'd built through IIT, Merrill Lynch, and New York finance – people who had seen him under pressure and seen him follow through. Ravi reached for a different set: friends from Washington University, Hyderabad classmates, former colleagues from his tech roles. The calls weren't dressed up as a "raise." They were direct: We're moving back to India to start something in mobile. We see the shift coming; we think we can meet it. Here's what we don't have yet.

The reactions were cautious but engaged. Many asked the same three questions: What problem are you solving? Why now? Why you? They answered without hedging the risk. Mobile was going to be the primary device for internet access in India. Publishers would need tools to adapt fast. Between Ravi's engineering depth and Sharat's business and finance experience, they believed they could build the bridge.

The earliest commitments came from Ravi's two friends and a clutch of IITM alumni, and from the New York circle Sharat had built. Jitamitra (now at IIMB) and Aparna wrote a check. Nandita and her husband invested. The most atypical came later from their first employee Shivnash Tyagi, whose father – an agriculturist with no tech background – put in ₹10 lakh. That money has grown roughly 40x, but what mattered then was the vote of confidence.

Both founders matched what they raised with their own savings. It wasn't a war chest; it was a finite pool of belief. Every choice had to pass a private test: will this justify the trust they've placed in us?

That knowledge seeped into early decisions. Hiring was slow and deliberate. Features were argued over before developer time was committed. Travel budgets were scrutinized. Every choice had to pass a simple, private test: Will this justify the trust they've placed in us?

It wasn't a war chest. It was a finite pool of belief. And that made it sharper.

The first checks were not venture capital. They came from classmates, colleagues, friends – people they would have to face if it failed.

EARLY HIGHS, HIDDEN CRACKS

When they sat down to decide what MobStac's first product would be, the filter was simple: ride a wave that was already gathering force. "Why now is the most important question," Sharat says. "In life you have to be at the right place at the right time. The easier way is, you see a river, you put hands and turn it into your kitty." The river, in 2010, was mobile.

The logic was straightforward. In India, the first thing most people did online was read news. But the experience on a phone screen was terrible: clumsy pinch-zooms, broken layouts, endless scrolling. If they could give publishers a way to deliver clean, fast mobile pages without rebuilding from scratch, they could make themselves indispensable.

The first big break came through a combination of hustle and proximity. Sharat reached into every contact list he had – IIT friends, family acquaintances, cold intros – and landed The Hindu as their first paying customer, at about ₹20,000 a month. "And then Deccan Herald, Times Properties, Mint...one by one," he says. It wasn't glamorous. It was calls, follow-ups, showing up in person.

The product began to spread in smaller, less visible ways. Ravi opened up a self-service version for bloggers, a kind of free distribution engine. Sharat mined the blogs for leads – "I would go through and email them one by one" – and each deployment carried a small but public signature: powered by MobStac. It was a quiet form of marketing, building familiarity before they ever walked into a publisher's office.

The real charge came from seeing the product in the wild. "I was on a flight, and the guy next to me was reading *The Hindu* on his phone," Sharat says. "I had a dying urge to tell him, I am powering that." It was a kind of validation that numbers couldn't touch. Ravi felt the same in New York when he scanned random QR codes – a later pivot – just to see if they were his. "One-fourth of the time, they are ours," he says.

They called it "groundswell," and it worked on two levels. In private, it was proof the product was being used – the moment an engineer or founder could point and say, "That's ours." In public, it was the subtle brand lift that came from recognizable names and media mentions. "Nothing gives more pleasure than telling the team this person is using it," Sharat says. "No Diwali bonus could have given as much joy."

The early wins masked deeper problems that would surface later, but in those first years, groundswell was fuel. It kept the team believing in the bet they had made – and, just as importantly, made it visible to the friends and family whose money was in the bank.

FAILURE BY A THOUSAND PAPER CUTS

The first phase of MobStac didn't collapse with a single blow. It bled out in a hundred small ways – the "failure by a thousand paper cuts" that Sharat says is harder to face than a clean break. "It's never black and white," he explains. "You keep telling yourself, maybe the pricing is wrong; maybe it's the feature set; maybe we're selling to the wrong ICP; maybe it's me, maybe I need to hand it to another salesperson. You keep plugging one hole after another."

By late 2013, the list of maybes was longer than the pipeline. Responsive web design was eating away at their wedge. Larger CMS platforms were integrating mobile capabilities by default. The customers still signing contracts were often doing it for the wrong reason. "If you're asking whether you have product-market fit," Sharat says now, "you don't have it."

It was Ravi who finally put it in an email that cut through the drift: You have to park yourself in New York and make a few sales. We can't sell from here. They had always respected each other's lanes – Ravi on product and post-sale delivery, Sharat on sales and fundraising – but this was not about jurisdiction. It was survival.

Sharat went. He pitched from borrowed conference rooms to enterprise prospects like Condé Nast and The Washington Post. The interest was polite until the demos started. Features lagged. Apps froze. Sometimes the software wouldn't load at all. Each failure triggered a late-night call back to Bangalore.

Ravi was blunt about what needed to happen: infrastructure first, new features second. They hired an outside DevOps team to shore up the platform, a cost they'd resisted until the broken demos made delay impossible. "It wasn't just embarrassment," Ravi recalls. "You realize the thing you're promising can't stand in the market you're trying to sell into."

The trip didn't rescue the business. What it did was reestablish the loop between promise and reality. Sharat could no longer sell in the abstract; Ravi could no longer postpone the fixes behind the firewall. Each knew exactly what the other was facing, in the same week, from opposite continents.

When they talk about it now, there's no nostalgia in their tone. Just the recognition that the email, the trip, and the broken demos were the moment the denial ended. The product wasn't going to scale. The only question left was what to do next – and how to end this phase without burning what they'd built.

"Take a hard look at the numbers."

THE FALL

By early 2015, MobStac was back where it had started in 2009 – only heavier. Six years earlier, Sharat and Ravi had been two greenhorns with little more than savings and pride on the line. Now they had forty-plus people on payroll, an expensive office, and a product whose market was shrinking under them.

The cracks had been widening for years. Responsive design and integrated CMS platforms had eroded their wedge. Broken demos in New York had exposed how fragile the infrastructure really was. By the time Sharat sent Ravi the blunt message – "It won't scale" – the truth was unavoidable.

Investor reviews turned from cautious to skeptical. The MRR slide went up but never enough. In one meeting, someone said it out loud: "At your age, you could make more in the market." Neither founder thought of themselves as old, but the subtext was clear: take the safe option, go get jobs.

The hardest choice wasn't whether to end MobStac's publishing line. It was how. Most founders in their position would have pulled the plug overnight, cut customers loose, and redirected engineers to the next bet. Sharat and Ravi refused to do that. They decided to end deliberately, to leave the field without burning the ground behind them.

Their last major customer was The Hindu. They gave the paper six months' notice – an eternity in the industry – and promised a full migration: code, configurations, operational support. In return, the paper agreed to a final payment that bought the founders just enough runway to keep their team intact while they searched for the next problem to solve.

It was not glamorous work. Multiple visits to The Hindu's office. Drafts of legal handovers. Quietly redeploying engineers off the old product while making sure support never slipped. No spin, no press release – just the methodical unwinding of something they had once believed would define their careers.

Privately, it was brutal. In Bangalore, Sharat sat at his kitchen table at 3 a.m., recalculating survival in weeks, not months, while Sowmya slept in the next room. In New York, Ravi dialed into investor calls from a co-working booth, the phone warm in his hand, listening to the same subtext: Why not quit?

They never said it aloud to each other, but they both knew: they were at the end of one story, with no guarantee another would begin. Sharat later described it in the language of heartbreak: "It's like after being divorced you are going back into the dating scene. In the old relationship, you had a shared life. In the new one, you have nothing to offer except that you'd once been married – and it hadn't worked out." Ravi added his sting: "You are asking others to try you because you have failed really well."

The only clean victory was The Hindu handover. It preserved a relationship, salvaged some cash, and left their credibility intact. Everything else was loss: market, momentum, morale. But in that wreckage lay a principle that would guide their rebuild – no zombie businesses, no half-measures. Every engineer, every sales call, every rupee would be pointed at what came next.

Advice came thick in those months – pivots to "hot" markets, polished slideware, fixes no customer wanted. "It was noise," Sharat says.

One voice stood out. George Zacharias, an advisor who had seen them through both highs and lows, offered no list, just a line: "Stop chasing shiny objects. Solve one big problem." It wasn't pep talk. It was an audit.

From then on, the filter was brutal. If an idea didn't clear the "big problem" bar, it died. That discipline set up their second act: bridging physical and digital, first through beacons, later QR codes and geofencing – without rebuilding each time.

Ravi put it bluntly: "We had one or two shots left. If it wasn't worth years, it wasn't worth doing."

Vidya noticed something else changing across the years: the length of the trough. "There was one time he was down for almost three weeks," she says. "We talked and he snapped out of it. Since then, the time the lows last has kept shrinking. The magnitude isn't smaller, but the recovery is faster."

It wasn't a happy ending. But it was an ending they could live with. And in startups, that can be the difference between starting over and never starting again.

REBUILDING UNDER CONSTRAINTS

The pivot out of publishing didn't feel like a fresh start. It felt like salvage. The headcount was down. Revenue had to be earned quarter by quarter. Every rupee was suddenly visible in a way it hadn't been when venture capital could blur the edges.

"When you have too much money, you can hide bad habits," Sharat says. "Now we had no cushion. Everything we did had to work."

The budgeting in those months wasn't symbolic. Rent, travel, software licenses – nothing escaped the filter: Will this get us closer to product-market fit or paying customers? If the answer wasn't yes, it didn't happen. A recruiter's fee could be justified; a conference booth could not. Even the smallest line items went under the same light. Ravi describes it as a muscle they hadn't used enough in the first act. "You think in years when the bank balance feels safe," he says. "Now we thought in quarters. Revenue wasn't a vanity metric – it was the metric."

That discipline reached into product decisions too. Features were judged not by elegance or novelty, but by whether they removed friction a customer would actually pay to avoid. The support rotation stayed in place – everyone who wrote code spent a week taking calls, screen-sharing, and logging issues. In that structure, the voice of the customer was never more than one conversation away from the next sprint.

A late-night WhatsApp from Accel's Shekhar Kirani landed in the middle of this reset: "No difference between you and the CEOs you admire – except they're on the other side of the climb." It wasn't capital, but it reframed the grind. The gap wasn't capability; it was endurance.

Day to day, the anchor was a WhatsApp group called "Wolf Gang," shared between the founders and a tight circle. It was venting and inspiration in equal measure – laughing when things broke, sharing pain when the grind bit hard, and lifting each other when someone was down. It was simply where they reminded each other to keep going.

By the time the new product began to take shape, the constraints had stopped feeling like punishment. They had become the operating system. "We learned to do without," Sharat says. "And that made us better at deciding what we actually needed."

The platform, piece by piece

The rebuild began with the one door that would open customer conversations: beacons. The hardware was never the point; the control layer was. Ravi kept repeating the same rule: stop asking what can we build – start where the pain is chronic and valuable.

The sequence was narrow by design:

- Use beacon hardware only because it unlocked the first proof-of-value calls.
- Build a SaaS control panel to configure, update, and measure those interactions.
- Add QR codes and NFC to the same platform, so every new access method plugged into a single codebase instead of spawning a new product line.
- Keep the control plane unified – one stack, multiple doors.
- Launch quietly. No headline chase. Ship, observe, adjust.

China → Bangalore → World. To earn early trust, they owned the last mile: import beacon hardware from China, configure and test in the Bangalore office, and ship worldwide in specially designed boxes. For a stretch, Beaconstac became one of FedEx India's larger SME customers, routing crores through that lane. The irony years later: FedEx itself became one of Uniqode's big customers.

Over time, the beacon became just a door. The platform was the house: one place to create and manage physical-to-digital connections, with usage and analytics in the same loop. When it made sense, geofencing was added the same way – an input to the control plane, not another business line.

The first enterprise logo that stuck was Nestlé. In U.S. conference rooms the Poland Spring bottle sat on almost every table; it became the most reliable ice-breaker in investor and customer meetings – QR and physical-to-digital, in a form everyone could touch.

LIFELINES

For all the talk of resilience as a personal trait, what Sharat and Ravi remember most about the pivot years is how much of it came from outside themselves. They can both name the moments, the people, and the gestures that made it possible to keep going when the logic of quitting was strong.

For Ravi, the first was Bhaskar, the neighborhood computer-center owner in Secunderabad, who took him in as a teenager struggling with maths and gave him a rule that still shapes how he works: don't just copy the code – change something and see what breaks.

For Sharat, the anchors were closer to home. Sowmya's belief – sometimes quieter, sometimes blunt – formed the backdrop to every 3 a.m. recalculation of runway. His parents' steady backing mattered more than any check. His father-in-law's refrain, "Keep at it," was simple, but it was a permission slip to continue when others were asking why he didn't take a safer path.

"In the early phases, I had a stable job and predictable hours," Vidya says. "That helped keep family life steady when his schedule was volatile." Later, as Uniqode stabilized and her own role grew more demanding, they traded notes across the divide—her big-company view, his startup view.

And then there were the people who sent their belief in a more tangible form. The $200,000 from Jayant Kadambi came with no deck, no negotiation, just a handshake over coffee. "Use this to make it work," Jayant said. It wasn't enough to buy comfort, but it was exactly enough to keep the lights on while they stripped away everything that wasn't essential.

The most atypical came from their first employee, Shivnash Tyagi, whose father – an agriculturist with no tech background – put in ₹10 lakh. That money has grown roughly 40x, but what mattered then was the vote of confidence.

For both founders, the point isn't that they survived because of one lucky break or one savior. It's that survival was a composite – built from moments when someone else's belief arrived just in time to bridge a gap they couldn't have crossed alone. The capital mattered. The counsel mattered. But most of all, the fact that someone had looked at them in the middle of the wreckage and decided they were still worth backing – that changed how they saw themselves in the fight.

SCARS AS MUSCLE MEMORY

For Sharat and Ravi, antifragility was never a philosophy they read and adopted. It was a posture forced by a decade of trial, attrition, and the quiet grind of making something work with less than it needed. They lived through enough reversals to see the pattern: setbacks weren't temporary detours, they were the work itself – material to be reused, reshaped, re-applied.

Some were sudden amputations. When Android deprecated the core feature that powered one of their products, the loss was immediate – no negotiation, no workaround. The WiFi-based app, WiFire, they had nurtured as an adjacent bet died the same way. In both cases, the failure stripped away months of work. The only way forward was to treat those months not as waste, but as R&D they'd been forced to run early.

Ravi talks about it in the language of iteration, not recovery: "If you're not embarrassed by what you were building twelve months ago, you're not learning fast enough." It's not a throwaway line; it's his operating benchmark. In his voice notes, he jokes that "iteration is my middle name," but the discipline behind the joke is hard-edged – try, discard, carry forward what holds up, repeat.

Sharat frames it through the lens of catastrophizing – a habit he has spent years naming and managing. Therapy at forty gave him a clearer sense of how often he defaulted to worst-case thinking, and how to use that reflex without letting it freeze him. Reading Taleb's *Antifragile* mid-flight one year, he underlined a passage on systems that gain from disorder. "Pain isn't optional," he wrote in the margin. "Growth from pain is."

Asked what she thinks is non-negotiable for founders, Vidya lists three: conviction, courage, and purpose. "There's no formula," she says. "You can read cases and biographies, but your story is your story."

They didn't turn every blow into a breakthrough. Some just left scars. But those scars became a kind of muscle memory – a quickened ability to strip a problem down to its load-bearing parts, to ignore the noise of sunk cost, to find a smaller, more durable core they could build from.

In the founders' WhatsApp thread, this mindset shows up as gallows humor and small wins logged without ceremony. A bug fix pushed at 1:12 a.m. after two weeks of dead ends. A QR code spotted in the wild that hadn't been in the last market sweep. No speeches, no post-mortems – just the quiet, cumulative work of getting better because the alternative is not to be here at all.

WHAT KEPT THEM GOING

For all their dashboards and board slides, the moments that kept the company alive rarely showed up on a chart.

When Sharat saw the man scrolling *The Hindu* on his phone, it wasn't revenue, but it was proof – the product existed in the world, being used by strangers.

Ravi describes the same impulse in Manhattan, scanning random QR codes on posters and billboards just to see if they were theirs. "One-fourth of the time, they are ours," he says. His children caught the habit too, pointing and shouting, "Nanna, QR code!" every time they spotted one. Absurd, domestic, sometimes comic – but each moment was a reminder that the work mattered.

Sometimes the validation came through his mobile phone. The U.S. support number didn't route to a call center. "It rang on my phone," Ravi says. "You hear the pain directly. It keeps you honest." Those calls weren't metrics, but they were their own kind of groundswell: proof that the product was real enough for someone to pick up the phone.

Public validation worked differently. When BusinessWorld or YourStory wrote about MobStac, it shifted how families and peers spoke about the company. Sowmya remembers her father clipping one article and saying for the first time, "Here is a smart guy; he may be successful." Ravi admits the stories didn't move the roadmap, but they changed conversations. "A mention in the press doesn't win you customers," he says, "but it buys you the chance to be heard." In a society where perception travels faster than fact, that mattered.

Sharat learned to separate the two. "Self-confidence is what I know I can do," he says. "Self-esteem is what I think others think of me." Both mattered, but they were not the same. Ravi put it more bluntly: "Iteration is my middle name." For him, the proof wasn't in headlines but in whether the next loop – bug, fix, release – landed better than the last.

Some celebrations had to be shaped around small children and long days. "When they completed ten years as founders, both families finally met at 9:30 or 10 p.m. for twenty minutes," Vidya says. "You're tired, but you still sit together and say: you did it."

Each sign mattered. A stranger reading *The Hindu* on his phone. A child pointing at a QR code. A support call on Ravi's phone. None of it showed up as revenue, but it was proof the work was real.

HOME SIGNALS

For Sharat, the hardest questions in recent years have not come from investors or customers. They have come from his children.

"Every day I feel like there are 25,000 things I could correct," he says. "The work is choosing which two matter." It is the same triage he recognizes from running a company: deciding which fires to let burn, which ones to put out, and which ones would consume the whole floor if ignored.

The debates at home mirror those in the office. With Sowmya, the axis is simple but unsparing: do you want to raise a happy child or a successful one? Sharat leans toward ambition, the drive that creates options. Sowmya insists on happiness first, arguing that ambition without joy is hollow. The argument itself is the calibration, the same way he and Ravi circle their Friday agenda until it lands in the middle ground that keeps the company moving.

Validation in parenting comes in smaller doses than a funding round or a signed contract. During one lean stretch, their son Ivaahn pressed a crumpled ten-rupee note into his mother's palm. "For the company," he said. The gesture was tiny, the intent exact: a child adding to the ledger. Months later, Sowmya received a photo from a friend at an airport – a stranger's child wearing Vobble headphones, her own company's product. The office went wild when she shared it. "These are the micro-validations you string together to keep going," she says.

Ravi recognizes the parallels in his own house. His children once mimicked his workday greeting – "Beaconstac support, this is Ravi" – turning it into a household joke. It was not glamor, but it was truth: the company had bled into family life in ways that were sometimes exhausting, sometimes comic, always undeniable.

Vidya extends the analogy in both directions. The highs exist too – hitting a revenue milestone feels like a child's first steps. And sometimes you have to let things flow: "You can't always analyze a market into behaving, just like you can't force a child into a love for tennis or a guitar. You try, you observe, and you decide when to pivot."

Parenthood, like founding, is not about control. It is about priorities. The measure is not whether everything is right, but whether enough of what matters survives to be built on tomorrow.

"One child pressed a ten-rupee note into his mother's hand. Another copied her father's support calls with a toy phone. These were the signals that mattered."

STILL IN THE RING

Early 2024. Both founders sit in their Manhattan office for a strategy review.

The meeting itself is unremarkable in form: dashboards on the screen, printouts on the table, talk about which markets to push harder, which features to retire, which bets to take again. Ten years earlier, reviews like this had been colored by dread – how many weeks of payroll were left, whether a broken demo could be salvaged, whether investors would walk. Now the questions are still demanding, but they begin from survival, not collapse.

Ravi points at a number on his laptop. "We'll change it again if we have to," he says. "That's the point."

Sharat nods once. "Still in the ring."

The words are not for effect. They carry the trail of what came before: nights of insomnia in Bangalore, support calls in New York, the divorce from a product that no longer fit, the bridge checks and WhatsApp bug threads, the ten-rupee note pressed into a parent's hand. Many founder pairs do not last this long. Most break on the rocks of ego, fatigue, or money. For them, the fact of still showing up together is the outcome.

If the Manhattan codes on the wall mark their public survival, the question behind them is simpler: how did this partnership last when most don't?

Survival is no longer theory – it shows up in the fact that both are still here, still together. Every Friday, ninety minutes are reserved. No investors, no customers, no board – just the two of them, the week's hardest truths on the table. The pact made years ago in a New York flat holds: one builds, one sells, both accountable.

FRIDAY FOUNDERS

Every Friday, from 11:30 to 1:00, the slot is blocked. No investor call, no customer review, no board demand gets in the way. It is just Sharat and Ravi.

The form has not changed in a decade. A pre-read email goes first – sometimes long, sometimes clipped. Writing forces clarity; many drafts never get sent. But when one does, it carries the sharpest truths: what is working, what is failing, what one founder sees the other missing.

The conversations that follow are not polite. “Let’s not let it fester,” Sharat says often. Ravi answers by pulling the argument back to its core: What does the company need? What are you doing? What is the delta? They leave the room with a decision, even if it takes a week of circling.

That discipline is what has kept the bond from souring. No festering, no unspoken resentments, no softened truths. A company, they remind themselves, is not a family. “It is a sports team,” Ravi says. Teams run on standards, not sentiment. That means hiring vetoes, exits delivered cleanly, and no tolerance for drift – whether in product, in people, or in themselves.

The Friday slot is not romantic. It is operational. But it is why the pact first made in a small New York flat – one builds, one sells, both stay accountable – has lasted long enough to become a rarity in entrepreneurship: **a partnership that has not cracked.**

08

ONE ENGINEER'S WAR AGAINST CHAOS

How Akash Gupta rewired his life – and GreyOrange – through obsession and relentless repair

THE RAILWAY CLOCK

In Dibiyapur, a single railway track ran ten meters from the Gupta family's gate. At 5:30 a.m., every day without exception, Akash's father stepped out for his shift.

"Structure was life. It wasn't enforced. It just was," Akash says. In a railway colony, precision wasn't a choice; it was the environment. Trains did not wait. Schedules did not bend.

For Akash – who would later try to build machines that held up under pressure – this was the first system he knew: not code or robotics, but the discipline of timetables.

The order outside didn't translate inside his day. Moving from a school of two hundred to PCVN in Kanpur, where two thousand boys stood in morning assembly, erased him.

"I disappeared," he remembers. His marks held, but in the crowd he was unseen.

The computer lab became the counterweight. Dusty tables. A flickering CRT. BASIC commands in a notebook. With his friend Devvrat, he coded a crude Kaun Banega Crorepati game in GW-BASIC. It had no polish, but it ran.

"The machine listened. That was new," Akash says. If it broke, the mistake was his. If it ran, it was because he made it run.

School kept its own ledger of pride and cuts. His name went up as school captain. He topped Class 10. But Class 12 left its mark – six of them, in English.

"Everything else was ninety-seven or ninety-eight," he says. "That still stays with me."

Then came the JEE years: two years of prep, drills, memorization. No coding. No robotics.

"Two years," Akash says flatly. "I was alive, but I wasn't learning anything."

The spark went cold. It would take Pilani to bring it back – not in class, but in a robotics lab, when he saw a humanoid blink.

Dibiyapur to Kanpur

From the rhythm of trains outside his home in Dibiyapur to the sea of uniforms at PCVN in Kanpur, Akash saw order on the tracks and felt himself disappear in the assembly.

I disappeared. That's when
the lab became my world.

WHEN THE ROBOT BLINKED BACK

At BITS Pilani, the classrooms were ordinary. The robotics lab was the reason to stay.

The space was called AcYut Lab, after AcYut – Sanskrit for indestructible – the project that produced India's first student-built humanoid robot. It wasn't an official institute program. It was a corner of campus where students pooled motors, wires, and late nights.

Walking in and seeing a humanoid blink – eyes stuttering just enough to look alive – was ignition. The two dead years of JEE prep fell away. Akash was no longer memorizing; he was making.

The first test came quickly. He submitted a CAD drawing of a robotic part. A senior looked at it and refused to believe he had done it himself.

"He didn't believe I made it. I left," Akash recalls. Pride met suspicion. He came back with cleaner drawings and more work. What followed wasn't recognition – it was momentum. Soon the challenge was set: "Let's win India's first medal in RoboGames with a humanoid."

From then on, the lab was home. "I only left to shower." His clothes stayed in someone else's room. Nights stretched into mornings. Sometimes the code compiled. Sometimes joints failed. The work went on regardless.

RoboGames in California made the world feel closer. A flight across the globe, a hall of strangers who cared about the same details, and the realization that Pilani and the global stage were separated only by effort. "I saw what building for the world could mean."

Some lessons didn't come from competition. They came in quieter places. In a garage in California, Raju Reddy, an entrepreneur who founded Sierra Atlantic, told Akash how he had started his company after leaving Intel.

"That story changed what I thought was possible," Akash says. Until then, entrepreneurship was something that happened elsewhere. Raju described it as steps: hire, ship, fix, ship again.

The AcYut lab gave Akash a place to belong. RoboGames and Raju's story gave him something else: a path out of the lab, into building for the world.

Let's build India's first humanoid.

BASEMENT HUNGER

By 2010, the robotics workshops that had paid their rent through college were over. Graduation left no buffer. What remained were a few skills, some leftover cash, and a harder question: what problem could become a company?

The first lesson came from the Indian Oil Corporation Limited. A proposal they submitted was lifted almost word for word into a tender – only to be awarded to someone else. "We learned – ideas mean nothing. Execution is the only language," Akash says.

The next lead came inside Flipkart's warehouse in Mahipalpur. The floor was noisy, hot, and chaotic. Packages were stacked everywhere. Workers tried to sort parcels by hand and kept falling behind.

"Sorting. That's the problem," Akash remembers. They left the warehouse, having promised a ₹70 lakh solution they had not yet built. "This could break us. We said yes anyway."

That yes had a price. They borrowed ₹40 lakh from Thomas Chance, a mentor from Akash's U.S. internship days, to buy a CNC – computer numerical control – machine. CNC machining was the only way to cut precision parts fast enough to meet the deadlines. "It was the dumbest – and best – decision we made," Akash says. None of them knew how to operate it. They learned by burning fingers on hot parts, re-machining broken joints, and rewriting control code until something worked. Many nights ended at three in the morning, with the machine still running.

The rest of the setup was no less improvised. "We had no money for proper furniture, so we bought tables and chairs from a Delhi flea market. We carried them in ourselves, assembled them with borrowed tools."

Support came from outside India too. In Mysore, after walking Wolfgang through a supply-chain automation plan, the German investor stayed late, asked questions, and finally said yes. He wired €100,000. "That wasn't applause," Akash says. "It was the survival capital." Enough to keep the lights on and the CNC running.

Soon after, Blume Ventures came in with GreyOrange's first institutional check. The money didn't make the work easier. But it made the company real.

GreyOrange began with a rejected tender, a chaotic warehouse, a loan for a machine that startups rarely thought of buying, and a late-night conversation in Mysore that ended with €100,000 wired into their account.

DE

HUMILIATION IN TOKYO, REDEMPTION IN DISNEY'S WAREHOUSE

Japan was GreyOrange's first foreign market, and it ended in significant learnings that came very hard. A customer rejected every unit from the first batch. There were no second chances. No debates. Just a quiet verdict that the machines had not met the standard.

Akash carried that lesson forward. If Japan showed them the cost of falling short of perfection, the United States became the place they had to prove they belonged.

The first step was winning a contract with XPO Logistics, one of the world's largest supply-chain operators. It wasn't symbolic. Breaking into a customer of that scale – where the standard was reliability under millions of shipments – was among the hardest markets in the world to enter.

Then came a Series C round. Ajay Royan at Mithril backed them, convinced by GreyMatter – their control software, written in Erlang. The choice of Erlang mattered: warehouses had hundreds of robots moving at once, and the language's concurrency meant the system could stay calm instead of crashing under load.

The bigger test wasn't on paper. It came inside Disney's warehouse during Cyber Monday peak. For sixty straight nights, Akash stayed there. He slept on site, ate at odd hours, stood by dashboards at 2 a.m., and stepped in when conveyors jammed.

That is how trust was built – not through slides or investor decks, but by being present when the system could either fail or survive. When the throughput held through the holiday rush, GreyOrange earned credibility.

The shame from Japan didn't disappear. The credibility in the U.S. didn't make the work lighter. It made it unavoidable.

"If you want to sell systems," Akash says, "you have to be the person who shows up when they fail – and you have to be ready for them not to fail the next time."

THE FRACTURE

The hardest blow didn't come from the market. It came from across the table.

Samay, the co-dreamer who had once pulled all-nighters in a Rajendra Nagar basement, voted no when the board asked who should lead GreyOrange next.

"That cut deeper than any competitor ever did," Akash recalls.

The years leading up to that vote had already strained the company. Japan's need for perfection had its toll on the company. In the United States, Akash spent sixty nights inside Disney's warehouse during the Cyber Monday peak. "I became a pseudo warehouse manager," he says. That credibility with customers was real, but it widened the gap with Samay. Samay wanted faster bets on software. Budgets became battles. When Akash asked for more allocation to gStore, Samay refused.

Then the market turned. Post-Covid demand slumped, cash burned faster than they could raise, and $50 million in debt was coming due within couple of years. It was no longer about geography or growth. It was about survival.

Inside the boardroom, the fracture became official. For Akash, it wasn't about authority. It was about recognition. "I wasn't chosen. I have to earn it now," he says.

The damage went further. The board barely knew him. "I was just building. I didn't build relationships with the board. Samay's version of me was the board's version of me. That was my mistake."

The vote left him technically in charge but emotionally absent. For two years, he buried himself in execution, avoiding the bigger calls. GreyOrange was held together by survival instincts, not leadership.

It was Binny Bansal who cut through. In Austin, his advice was blunt: "Burn is killing you. Cut it in half. First, figure out how to survive."

That forced a reckoning. The fracture was not just between two co-founders. It was inside Akash himself. He could no longer hide in engineering. Leadership meant carrying the company's failures as his own – and deciding if he wanted to lead at all.

It was the moment GreyOrange stopped being a partnership. And the moment Akash had to choose if he wanted to be more than an engineer, and endure chaos.

That cut deeper than any competitor ever did.

DEATH BY PERPETUAL

There was a number GreyOrange could not ignore anymore: ₹400 crore. That was what had been burned.

There was another number: seven thousand robots. Every one of them shipped without a subscription. Each January, revenue reset to zero. Each December, it ended there again.

Akash is blunt: "We sold ₹400 crore of software and created little financial value. We didn't even know we were doing it."

They were not alone in the mistake. "Manhattan was full perpetual. AutoStore... perpetual." In the industry, one-time licenses were standard. For a venture-backed company, they were fatal. The contracts looked big, the deployments went live, but nothing compounded. Subscription revenue builds on itself; perpetual erases.

Inside GreyOrange, the machines ran. Customers used them. Invoices were paid. But the commercial model stripped away the very thing that survival depended on: recurring revenue.

The reckoning was real, not abstract. Selling robots on one-time licenses meant every January the company reset to zero, no matter how many systems it had installed the year before. It was an endless chase – close new orders or run out of cash. There was no compounding base to stand on.

Akash later described the pivot this way: "It's almost like you are doing well, and then suddenly, you are going into the valley of death. But it's a good decision because you get a fairly large recurring revenue base, which is a lot more valuable and sustainable, eventually."

By 2019-2020, GreyOrange rebuilt the company almost from scratch, ripping apart the perpetual model that had brought in break-even revenue and starting again with subscriptions. "Nothing comes today from the business models that gave us revenue in the first five years," Akash says.

Fixing this wasn't about writing a new strategy document. It meant changing everything: the code, the contracts, the culture of how GreyOrange sold. The answer took shape in adding gStore to the product portfolio – its first pure subscription-based software platform.

Akash built it the hard way, spending months inside COS retail stores in Beverly Hills, watching how floor staff moved products, where bottlenecks appeared, and how software could make the whole system reliable. The model was different: don't sell once and walk away, sell so that customers keep paying because the system keeps working.

Unlike the robots, it was not sold once. It was sold to be renewed.

"Revenue that remembers you showed up last year, and expects you to show up again."

CULTURAL BREAKAGE

Changing a product is hard. Changing pride is harder.

For a decade, GreyOrange's engineers had built machines from scratch – chassis, joints, vision systems – the pride of being the team that could make metal move. That pride was its own identity: we are the company that builds.

Parallelly, GreyMatter evolved into subscription-based software platform as well. Instead of building every robot in-house, the job was to orchestrate many – integrating machines from other manufacturers and making sure warehouses ran reliably on a single system.

Opening the GreyMatter platform to third-party robots made the cultural break sharper. It meant asking engineers who had built bots for years to now validate machines built elsewhere. "Why should I be the one validating someone else's robot?" Akash recalls hearing. "I understood it. But I had to move."

The shift landed as an insult to some.

"It felt like betrayal to them," Akash says. "These were people who had built robots for a decade. I had to rebuild the complete team and culture."

The cultural fracture wasn't about job descriptions. It was about what GreyOrange was. A robotics company measured by how many robots it built – or a software company measured by how reliably warehouses ran. gStore made the answer unavoidable.

The reckoning extended beyond people. GreyOrange kept a manufacturing unit alive as a fallback against U.S.-China tariffs. On paper, it was insurance. In practice, it was indecision.

"If tariffs spike, we're underwater. But we can't keep living in backup mode forever," Akash says. "I've kept the unit alive just in case. But that's a mindset problem too. I need to shut the door completely or this company will never be clean."

These weren't cosmetic changes. The old GreyOrange could build elegant machines, but not a compounding business. The new GreyOrange would only survive if it rewired its pride – away from how many robots it produced, and toward whether customers renewed their trust.

Akash puts it simply: "We didn't pivot the *Titanic*. We built a dinghy next to it."

THE REBUILD AS BREATH

After a decade of firefighting, 2024 did not begin with momentum. It began with oxygen. GreyOrange had survived the fracture with Samay, the weight of debt, and the reckoning with perpetual software. It hadn't collapsed. But it hadn't healed either.

The difference was posture. For the first time, Akash stopped operating like a machine in execution mode. The company's rhythm shifted from chasing speed to proving stability – from surviving the month to repeating outcomes customers could rely on.

The dashboards made the shift visible. gStore crossed $12 million in contracted annual recurring revenue. There was no launch, no fanfare.

"No launch. No noise. But it worked," Akash says.

That alignment reshaped everything downstream. Go-to-market decks were rewritten, stripping away talk of "the future of robotics" and grounding messaging in lived performance: warehouses run, peak season handled, customers renew. Akash was blunt:

"In this space, people don't buy the future. They buy reliability. 'Have you done this before?' is more important than 'How innovative is it?'"

The rebuild was not reinvention. It was recognition – that what mattered was compounding trust, one expansion at a time. Customers who once asked for novelty now asked a different question: will the system still work when the volume doubles? GreyOrange, for the first time in years, could answer yes without hesitation.

"It's what GreyOrange should have always been," Akash says. "Simple product. Clear use case. Recurring revenue."

A call with customers ended without applause or theatrics, but with something better: partnership. "Now we're not just surviving. We're compounding."

Akash later admitted that the pivot felt like tearing the company apart twice. "We literally built a company to the point of achieving breakeven and then completely ripped it apart. In 2019-2020, we started building it again. Nothing today comes from the business models that gave us revenue in the first five years."

For him, the rebuild wasn't about new features or flashy launches. It was about customers staying because the system worked, month after month.

AFTER SURVIVAL, THEN WHAT?

For years, GreyOrange lived inside the math of survival. Every call was about runway, every week about whether the burn could be slowed, every plan shaped by debt that never left the dashboard. That posture carried its own danger: when you survive too long, you start to mistake survival for the job itself.

By 2024, the equation had changed. Warehouses were running. gStore revenue was recurring. The panic had eased. That did not mean GreyOrange was safe – it meant the company finally had the right to ask a harder question: what now?

One answer came in New York. Akash walked investors through a $250 million ARR plan. The motive wasn't theater. "Not because we need to go public. But because we finally can," he said. Years of constraint had narrowed every decision: cut costs, stretch runway, make the next payroll. When the constraint lifted, the frame shifted.

"That was the moment I stopped thinking about fixing GreyOrange. And started thinking – what can this become?"

The reset wasn't an end to responsibility. It was its expansion. GreyOrange had been patched and repaired into functionality. Now it had to decide what to build, which markets to serve, and what role to claim in a global supply chain where credibility was finally within reach.

Akash put the baseline in plain words: "We will never run out of cash again. But now I start again."

The years of near-death had bought them a second chance.

"It was almost like walking into the valley of death twice," Akash says of the SaaS transition. "But if you survive it, you end up with a recurring base that is far more valuable and sustainable."

By the time he walked into the New York investor meeting with the $250 million plan, the foundation was different. GreyOrange wasn't a robotics vendor anymore. It was a platform company tied together through subscription.

The reset was the acceptance that not dying is not the work. The work is to matter.

SCAR TISSUE

The last image isn't grand. A whiteboard. Two columns: Scale and Repair. One tick mark: Still here. It looks like maintenance, because it is.

The truths Akash repeats don't sound like strategy. "Startups don't die because of competition. They die when the founder forgets why he started." The memory of why matters more than any slide deck – remember the problem, remember how the system fails under load, remember the promises you can actually keep.

What changed wasn't only GreyOrange's wiring. It was Akash. "I thought the hard part was building machines. It wasn't. The hard part was becoming someone who could lead people through chaos – without breaking." That change came slow, and not without damage. "For two years, I was technically in charge but emotionally absent," he admits. After the fracture with Samay, he buried himself in execution. The company kept moving, but not because of leadership. It was survival instinct, stretched thin. That gap, and the repair it forced, is what left scar tissue.

Now the company and the founder carry the same inheritance: less flexible than before, harder to tear, stronger in the places where they once failed.

Today, the panic is gone. Warehouses run and stores thrive. The team doesn't need a founder on a plane every week to keep throughput honest. That doesn't make the work smaller. It makes the questions sharper: what do we really solve, what does survival unlock, who are we when nothing is on fire.

The constraint that defined the last chapter – just staying alive – is over. A new one replaces it: purpose. "We'll never run out of cash again. But that just means I have to figure out what actually matters."

And even now, Akash doesn't call this success. He calls it a work in progress.

Stability is not the end. It is only the ground for the next set of mistakes – and the resilience that must follow. In startups, repair is never closure. It is the beginning of the next chapter.

09

THE MIDNIGHT CHASE

The reluctant CEO: Kartheeswaran KK and the survival of Ninjacart

The Last One to Try

Kartheeswaran KK was not supposed to be here. By any middle-class script, his story should have ended at Microsoft or a consulting firm – loans cleared, stability secured. Instead, at two in the morning, he was slumped in the passenger seat of a hatchback, chasing the taillights of a vegetable truck. A notebook balanced on his knees, pen scratching every time the lorry swerved.

This was not exploration. It was survival. Ninjacart had already pivoted twice, and the numbers still bled. Discounts vanished, margins collapsed. Every other founder had tried to fix sourcing and failed. KK was the last one left.

The highways around Madiwala carried more than produce. They carried the question that stalked him through nights of diesel smoke and stiff-necked naps: Was the company he had staked his life on even a business at all?

"If I failed," he would say later, "it wasn't just me. It was existential."

WHY WE WERE NOT MAKING MONEY

The nights blurred into each other. The sour–sweet stench of vegetables mixed with diesel smoke at Madiwala market clinging to KK's clothes long after he got home. More than once, he had to tail the trucks for a hundred kilometers just to learn where the load had really come from.

Most drivers brushed him off. Others lied. He would wake with a stiff neck under the harsh yellow glow of street lamps, chasing dead ends. The exhaustion was real, but the fear that drove him was sharper.

Ninjacart had already pivoted from consumers to kirana stores. They had run discounts. They had chased growth. But none of it held. Margins vanished, dashboards looked good for a week only to collapse the next. Somewhere between the farm, the trader, and the retailer, the money was leaking out.

By then, every co-founder had tried and failed. Thiru had tried sourcing. Sharath had tried. Vasu had tried. Now it was KK's turn.

That word wasn't an exaggeration. Salaries had to be paid. Loans already weighed on him. If he couldn't figure out where the economics broke, the company itself could die.

So he kept chasing. Night after night, highways unspooling under high beams, notebooks filling with fragments, the fear circling tighter each time he hit another dead end. Until only the brutal question remained:

Why was Ninjacart still not making money?

FOUNDATION: WHERE KNOWLEDGE BECOMES POWER

KK was eight when he lost his mother. The house in Erode, Tamil Nadu, fell silent. His father, shattered, drifted through those days in grief. It was his grandfather who stepped forward, waking him before dawn for temple rounds on Saturdays, taking him to the rice mill and the Sunday market, insisting only on one thing: study well.

"He played on the front foot," KK said. "That trait came from him, not my father."

Front foot meant you didn't retreat when life collapsed. You faced the blow, head-on. His grandfather had done it before: marrying off five daughters in an era that dismissed women's education, even pawning his wife's jewelry to buy tractors, expand fields, and start a rice mill. For KK, those mornings watching him sell rice at the market or pray at temples weren't rituals. They were lessons in resilience, in living life full-blown, in refusing to be cowed by loss.

Later, another moment sealed a different truth. One morning, a wealthy uncle sat in their modest living room, consulting his father. His father was not only a government banker by profession, but also a chartered accountant. To see a man of means lean on his father for guidance, humbly, imprinted a conviction in KK that never left him: wealth bends to knowledge.

"Knowledge is respect. Knowledge is power," he realized.

At Guindy, in late-night dorm rooms littered with coffee cups and patent forms, KK carried those twin inheritances – front foot boldness and reverence for knowledge. With friends, he built an authentication product, even filed for a patent. But when the application stalled, another crack appeared in the neat ledger his father kept back home.

"Though I can build things, if we can't put it to real use, there is no real impact."

For his father, stability was the goal. A secure job, rupees accounted for, no risks that could undo years of discipline. For KK, shaped by loss, by his grandfather's defiance, by the sight of wealth bowing to knowledge, the lesson was harsher: knowledge mattered most when it was put to work, and impact demanded stepping up, front foot.

I WON'T SELL SOAPS AND SHAMPOOS

At Microsoft, KK's internship was meant to be the safe path. The cubicles were spotless, the processes airtight, the salaries unmatched. But for him, it felt like suffocation. "I wanted to learn fast," he recalled. "But the pace was too slow in the team." Work trickled through endless meetings; urgency was absent.

When final placements came at IIM Ahmedabad, the Microsoft offer was on the table. Solid, enviable. The middle-class dream. But KK didn't get the role he wanted, and by then, he no longer wanted the life it represented.

The conviction had been forming for months. One evening in the IIMA auditorium, he listened to Sanjeev Bikhchandani of Naukri.com and Venkat Krishnan of GiveIndia. They spoke of building from scratch, of organizations measured not in brands but in the impact they left behind. The words cut through the noise of placements and packages. Stability without meaning was emptiness.

"After IIMA, I knew one thing clearly," KK said. "I won't sell soaps and shampoos. I had to build something with real impact."

Back home in Erode, his father was baffled. For him, Microsoft was the finish line of decades of discipline. The brand, the salary, the security he had counted rupee by rupee. For KK, it was the opposite. To take that offer would have been to step away from the "front foot" his grandfather had taught him to play.

The Microsoft letter stayed untouched, a symbol of two clashing worldviews: one that equated success with stability, and another restless for meaning.

For KK, it also marked a line of no return. If he was going to reject stability, then there was no place for half-measures. "Don't do patchy work," he told himself. "Be whatever the company wants you to be. Go all in."

THE REAL MBA

The Bravo card came six months into TaxiForSure. A slip of paper, handed to KK almost casually at the end of a meeting: "For the person who feels the work he does, keep up the good spirit." For most, it was a token. For him, it was a door.

He walked straight to Raghu, card in hand. "This is nice," he said. "But give me half an hour every week. I want to learn from you." Raghu agreed.

Those lunches and Saturday chats became KK's real MBA. He had to catch Raghu in the right mood. Sometimes over a crowded team lunch, other times when Raghu sat alone on a beanbag on a weekend. KK would slip in questions, blunt ones no case study had prepared him for.

Why was Ola growing like wildfire while they debated efficiency? Why hire such a strange mix of city heads – army veterans, FMCG managers, IIM grads? Why swing from chasing profit to chasing growth, seemingly overnight?

Raghu's answers were unvarnished. "Domain is overrated. Play to your strengths. Hire for conviction, not pedigree." Another time, watching Ola outpace them, he said simply: "Speed over efficiency. Don't waste time building the perfect system. Get to market. Adapt later."

The lessons weren't only theoretical. One night in Delhi, a developer's script error debited instead of crediting driver wallets. By morning, over a thousand furious drivers surrounded the office. Phones buzzed with threats. A colleague screamed at KK: "What have you done? I'm about to get beaten up!" KK froze, convinced his job was over.

Raghu didn't fire him. Instead, he said the line that KK would carry into every crisis that followed: "If your intentions are right, you can take risks."

It was liberating. Failure wasn't the end. It was tuition.

Years later, when KK chased produce trucks at 2 a.m., when pivots forced him to fire people, when margins collapsed, he returned to Raghu's tests: Were the intentions right? Was speed greater than polish? If yes, the risk was worth it.

Looking back, he called it his "real MBA." Not in Ahmedabad classrooms, but in the Bravo card, the angry drivers, the blunt one-liners. Lessons hard-earned, paid for not with tuition but with scars.

The Bravo card was no token. It was the door to Raghu's blunt truths, lessons KK still calls his real MBA.

THE FOUNDER OF SHOUT

KK had admired Thiru's product instincts long before he knew the backstory. At TaxiForSure, Thiru wasn't the type to sit in the office – he was out with drivers and customers, absorbing problems firsthand. KK had quietly learned product management from him. Only later, over lunch, did he discover that Thiru had also built Shout, a locality-based Twitter app he'd been using himself. Thiru never led with that credential. KK's respect came first from watching him work – the Shout revelation only compounded it.

THE RECCE

Vasu didn't walk into his TaxiForSure interview cold. The day before, he had slipped into the Delhi operations office and spent hours observing dashboards, driver behavior, and call center flows. At the interview, when asked detailed questions, he rattled off insights no outsider could possibly have known. When pressed, he admitted he had "spent the day in your ops office." The brazenness was shocking, but it revealed a rare hunger. KK was struck: this wasn't an ordinary candidate.

He literally did a recce before joining.

THE NEGOTIATOR

Sharath had always been the hustler. Back in his EduRaft days with Thiru, he had once sold a school software product before it even existed, collecting a one-lakh check upfront and forcing Thiru to build under pressure. At Ninjacart's earliest days, the same instinct surfaced. Vendors opened negotiations at ₹100 per delivery. Sharath pressed, paused, sensed their desperation, and closed at ₹7. KK, listening from the next cabin, was stunned. This wasn't rational bargaining – it was a gift for flipping the power in a deal.

He cracked a deal at ₹7 per delivery.

THE TEAM

When Ninjacart began, the four founders knew they weren't enough. They had no money to buy "great talent." What they could afford was drive. KK went back to Guindy, his undergrad campus, and started pulling in juniors. He told them plainly: "You'll get ₹30,000 at CTS or TCS. I can pay you the same. But here, in one year, you'll learn what you can't learn anywhere else."

He didn't look for marks. He looked for people who had done something outside exams – run the tech fest, organized events, built small projects. Even those carrying arrears but showing hunger were taken in. To his surprise, many said yes. They joined for learning, not for safety. A decade later, some of those same juniors still run major charters inside the company – heads of supply chain, category, and more.

The second wave came after the first fundraise. A million-dollar check changed the risk profile. Now KK could pull in close friends he had always trusted. People with real skills in sales, supply chain, technology. "These were the guys I would have started off with if I hadn't found Thiru, Vasu, and Sharath," he said. One by one, they joined, and brought in more references of their own. The circle widened – no longer four founders trying to will a company into existence, but a cohort of believers, each one taking the same bet.

The third wave never ended. To build a large company in a large ecosystem, Ninjacart could not afford to get stuck chasing résumés. "Reliance or More had people in the fresh category," KK said once, "but they weren't reinventing anything. We needed people who would." In the early years, they hired generalists who could do anything because the company itself didn't know yet what it would become. Later, as functions matured, specialists followed. But the rule stayed constant: hire for drive first.

Looking back, KK put it bluntly: "We realized early – four of us wasn't enough. We had to invest in the team that counts."

That conviction carried them through pivots, through humiliations in shops, through nights of chasing trucks. What kept Ninjacart alive wasn't just the founders. It was the widening circle of people who believed in them enough to stake their lives. That belief, more than capital, became the company's true engine.

THE POINT OF NO RETURN

At the bank that morning, KK held in his hands a check larger than anything he had ever seen: ₹15 lakh, his TaxiForSure ESOP payout. He remembers lifting it over his head, half in disbelief, half in pride. "Fifteen lakh, sir. Have you ever seen it in real life?" he would laugh later. For a middle-class kid from Erode still carrying the weight of an IIMA education loan, this was supposed to be closure. "This is my education loan closure," he thought, even taking a photo with the check.

His father's words rang in his ears: "You are in your first job and already earning equal to what I earned at the end of my career. If you quit, be absolutely sure about why." For his father's generation, a check like this was the finish line. It was the financial safety net, the reward after decades of discipline.

But that same night, the reality at Ninjacart broke through. Salaries were due. Sellers were pressing. Thiru called, saying Vasu and Sharath were at his place, panicked that they had no money to pay suppliers the next morning. The company would not survive the week without cash.

KK had a choice: close his education loan and secure his personal future, or wire the entire check into Ninjacart. He didn't even tell his father what he was about to do. "The TFS ESOP money was supposed to close my education loan," he said later. "Instead, I put it into Ninjacart because we had to survive."

It was not heroic. There was no term sheet, no headline. Just a quiet, irreversible crossing of a line: choosing the company's life over his own safety net.

For his father, loans were only for absolute necessities a home, a child's education, something guaranteed to outlast the sacrifice. KK had used his one chance at repayment for the opposite: to buy a few more months of life for a company still stumbling through pivots.

The loan remained for years. But the check had already done its work. It bound him tighter to Ninjacart, turning survival from a preference into a necessity. From that moment, the road back closed.

THE DISCOUNT COMPANY

The dashboards told a story that looked like triumph. Three thousand orders a day, drivers rushing across the city, green arrows rising. For a brief moment, it felt as if the gamble – the ₹15 lakh check, the long nights, the brotherhood – had bought them liftoff.

Then one change stripped the illusion bare. Cut the discount by fifty rupees, and orders collapsed to five hundred.

"We weren't a business," KK admitted later. "We were a discount company."

The collapse showed up everywhere. At the call center, customers shouted about bags missing atta, wrong substitutions, deliveries that never arrived. In the kirana shops, anger boiled over. One shopkeeper hurled a ten-rupee note at KK and snapped: "Just take this and get out." The sting of that gesture cut deeper than any chart on a dashboard.

The founders could no longer hide behind optimism. They had told themselves scale was around the corner, that burn was justified as long as growth climbed. But the numbers told the truth. They weren't building a company; they were burning one.

The bluntest reckoning came from Subrata Mitra, over dinner at his table. He listened quietly: "I like the team. But this idea won't work. Don't exhaust all the money." KK needed to hear that.

It was the hardest truth of all – that grit, sacrifice, even the ₹15 lakh check meant nothing if the economics didn't work. Brotherhood alone couldn't save them from arithmetic.

That was the day they knew. The company they thought they had built was already gone. What lay ahead wasn't refinement but reinvention.

And so survival moved to the highways. The pivot they had skirted around became unavoidable. If Ninjacart was to live, someone had to chase the trucks, map the routes, and find where the real margins were hiding.

IF I FAILED, IT WAS EXISTENTIAL

"There were nights we chased trucks for a hundred kilometers."

"I was the last co-founder to attempt farmer sourcing," he recalled. "If I failed, it wasn't just me – it was existential."

Week after week, the pattern repeated. Out of Bangalore, jolting awake as the car swerved around potholes. Cornering drivers at roadside stalls, asking questions that met with shrugs or outright lies. Each dead end deepened the fear that this might be the stretch where Ninjacart finally ran out of time. Salaries, loans, and months of sacrifice hung on these night hunts.

And then, slowly, the notebook began to tell a different story. The assumption had always been that Bangalore's vegetables came from the surrounding villages. But the scribbled routes revealed something else: tomatoes hauled in from Maharashtra, onions from Nashik, cucumbers from Mandya. The city's markets weren't local at all. They were nodes in a shifting national web, moving with season and demand.

"We thought we understood our market," KK admitted. "But we didn't even know its real scale."

What began as futility turned into clarity. The trucks weren't just vehicles; they were maps. The problem wasn't impossible. It demanded building a network as sprawling and dynamic as the supply routes themselves.

That realization became the bridge to everything that followed. Once the truth of scale was visible, the next steps – apples from Turkey one month, Poland the next; shifting from manual phone calls to ML-driven sourcing; even the company's own inside joke, "May the Source be with you" – all of it flowed from these notebooks.

Somewhere between fatigue and fear, in the silence of those highways, KK found what he had been chasing. Failure hadn't crushed him. It had given him the one truth that mattered: survival was still possible.

PROGRESS IS THE BEST STORYTELLER

Titles had never mattered much to KK. COO wasn't something he was given; it was something he grew into. He had carried vegetables at dawn, chased trucks at night, argued with shopkeepers, sat with drivers at dhabas. By the time he was officially COO, everyone already knew he had earned it.

But CEO was different. That title arrived not through years of ground work, but through a vacuum. In 2020, when Thiru fell ill and stepped back for stretches, KK found himself filling the role by default. The company needed someone in front, someone to face the board, someone to keep the machine moving. He did it – but inside he couldn't silence the voice that said: this wasn't mine.

"I always felt COO I earned," he admitted. "CEO, I didn't earn."

Every board review, every investor call carried a double weight. Progress reports on one hand, and on the other, the suspicion that he was carrying a mantle he hadn't proven worthy of. COO was sweat and scars you could show. CEO was expectation, and an unease he couldn't shake.

It became one of the loneliest passages of his journey. COO was earned in mandis and markets; CEO arrived in hospital corridors and boardrooms. One felt like his skin. The other felt borrowed.

He went back to the line that had anchored him across roles: "Be whatever the company wants you to be." It had already carried him from CTO to sales, to sourcing, to COO. Now it had to pull him once more. He could never be Thiru. He didn't need to be. He had to become a new version of himself.

"I can never become Thiru. I have to become a new me."

The push to step up wasn't abstract. It came at his lowest point. KK often linked it back to the moments that had shaped him: losing his mother at eight, and watching his grandfather step forward, "front foot," raising him and demanding only that he study well. "That trait came from my grandfather, not my father. He taught me to face blows head-on." Years later, he lost his mother again, this time to cancer. And then came Thiru's collapse, which he described as losing his mom all over again.

"I lost my mom once, I lost my mom again, and now I was losing Thiru. Why am I here? Why am I going through all this pain?"

The answer was the team. KK had personally hired hundreds. College juniors with arrears but drive, close friends who had taken risks, generalists who grew into specialists. They hadn't just joined a company; they had bet on him.

"They believed in my story and joined. How can I turn my back on them? If I ever see them in my life, can I tell them I was too coward to quit? No. I can die trying, but I won't live with that guilt."

That was his point of no return.

He leaned into what set him apart. Thiru had always been the natural storyteller, the voice in the room. KK never tried to match him there. He found his edge in action.

“I was not the best storyteller, Thiru was. So I played to my strengths: progress is the best storyteller.”

That line carried the company. Investors, employees, even himself – no one needed promises. They needed proof. A crate of apples arriving from the right country at the right price. A mandi going live in three days. A payment system that didn’t break. Progress steadied the board, lifted morale, and gave him credibility.

“Growth is infectious,” he told his team. “It changes morale more than words. Show progress.”

Not a coach on the sidelines, but a playing captain, walking the talk. Progress became the only story that counted.

THE MARATHON LENS

By the time Ninjacart crossed its first decade, KK's sense of time had changed. The early years were measured in quarters, in pivots, in dashboards glowing one week and collapsing the next. Now the unit was longer. Decades, not months.

He had lived through pivots, nights of chasing trucks down highways, and days of humiliation in stores. He had carried the weight of self-doubt through boardrooms, even hospitals during Covid. Each scar taught him that survival wasn't a sprint. It was about staying the course.

The shift came slowly, over years of exhaustion, illness, and personal change. He remembered his grandfather's "front foot" lesson after his mother's death at eight: life doesn't pause for grief, you move forward. That instinct kept him going in Ninjacart's hardest phases. But now, as a father himself, he felt another demand – balance.

"I'm not looking at this as a hundred-meter race anymore," he said. "It's a marathon. I know I'm building something great, so I have to give it that respect."

On Sundays in Bangalore, at a park with his child and a football, he understood the change most clearly. "It's not a stint," he said. "It's a part of my life." He no longer imagined finishing Ninjacart and moving on. It was woven into who he was, alongside being a son, a husband, and a father.

For KK, legacy was not about valuation or headlines. It was about progress. Sustained proof that farmers, retailers, and the team could carry the impact forward for decades. The company had to outlast its founders, and the founders had to outlast the company.

The sprint years had tested him. The marathon years, he now believed, would be his true measure.

BACK AT THE LAMP

Entrepreneurial Truths
Looking back on a decade, KK offered no sugarcoating, only what he called the truths that had kept him on the road when nothing else made sense.

Be whatever the company wants you to be.
He had lived that line – from writing code to chasing trucks, from COO to reluctant CEO – stepping in wherever survival demanded.

A startup is alive as long as its last founder believes.
Through pivots and breakdowns, he learned that the company doesn't die until the final founder gives up.

You owe it to the team that believed first.
He carried the weight of hundreds who had joined because they trusted him. That debt was heavier than any loan.

In the early innings, speed over efficiency.
TaxiForSure had taught him that lesson. Ola won by shipping faster, not cleaner. It was a scar he never forgot.

They were not slogans. They were scars turned into principles. For KK, they remain the only truths worth carrying forward.

HyperVerge

BEYOND THE LIMIT

"If money, society, and expectations are kept aside, what do we want to make happen in this world?" The journey of HyperVerge.

THE QUESTION

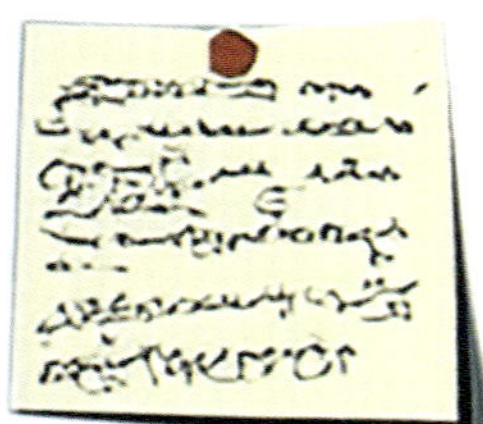

The bruises were still fresh. An AI-powered photo app, Silver, that the team had poured months into, was erased overnight when Google Photos launched. Google offered unlimited storage and made itself the default gallery app on every Android phone – crushing the fragile product before it could breathe.

In desperation, the team pivoted from utility to engagement. At Forum Mall, Kishore and his colleagues approached strangers with their app, only to face refusals. What stung deeper was watching some of the most brilliant IITM juniors – 9.9 and 9.4 pointers who had joined in good faith – spend endless hours designing face masks and filters meant not to solve problems, but to make users waste time.

The apps had failed to scale, but the underlying technology still carried value. By late 2016, multiple large tech companies had approached them with acquisition offers – a $10-12 million deal on the table. For engineers just two years out of college, it was a natural and tempting exit. Yet something resisted.

That December, they gathered in the pantry of IKP in Koramangala. For three long nights, the conversation circled around the same dilemma: should they sell and move on, or continue? Fluorescent lights hummed overhead. Plastic chairs scraped into a loose circle. On the wall, taped charts of downloads and growth targets – the vocabulary of investors – hung like reminders of borrowed goals. The air was heavy, not with strategy, but with silence.

At one point, Kedar picked up a marker and wrote on a bright Post-It: "If money, society, and expectations are kept aside, what do we want to make happen in this world? What would you invest your life energy into?"

He pinned it to the wall. The room fell silent again. Then he spoke, not offering comfort: "A group is what it stands for. Just because we enjoy working together doesn't make our work meaningful. If all of us are going to use our intelligence to waste users' time, then let's exit and part ways. If we want to come together to figure out how we can contribute to the world, then it makes sense to stay together."

The words landed heavy. But they also unlocked something. Slowly, the conversation shifted – from features and traction to intent and contribution. That night marked a new beginning, not only for the company, but for the people who chose to stay and build it.

Money and societal conditioning weren't a problem, what would you do with the rest of your life? What would you want to invest your life energy into?

MANY THREADS, ONE LOOM

IIT Madras had just set up its Center for Innovation (CFI), a maker-space where students built strange machines late into the night: a submersible plane, a self-balancing bicycle.

In 2009, Kedar started the Computer Vision Group (CVG). Sai was one of the first to join. Together they prepared for the International Aerial Robotics Competition – one of the toughest contests in the world. The summer of 2010 was brutal: Chennai heat, research papers they could barely parse, and code that broke more than it ran. Then, in a stroke of patience and brilliance, Sai cracked the breakthrough. The team became one of the top contenders globally. Sai went on to lead the club the next year, and quietly became its nucleus.

That December, he began teaching computer vision to more than fifty students at CFI. The juniors still remember it like a scene from a film: Sai at a glowing MacBook gifted by his uncle, algorithms flickering on screen, faces leaning in. By year's end, only four remained.

Two of them were KV and Kishore. Kishore was the earnest junior Sai bumped into every morning at 7 a.m. on the way to the washroom. KV came just to hang out, and ended up falling in love with computer vision.

By the following year, KV and Kishore were leading. They presented to an auditorium of seven hundred, then trained a room of fifty, and finally found five juniors who stayed: Hari, Nikhil, Prasanna, Adarsh, and Abhinav. KV could do in a night what might take the team a week. Kishore was different: he lived with the juniors, joked with them, slogged beside them. He was not a "senior"; he was a companion. Two of those juniors, Hari and Nikhil, are still with HyperVerge, thirteen years later.

Another character soon entered. Praveen, KV's roommate, was introduced simply as "a guy who can get any job done." At first, he was far removed from CVG's world. But over time, his instinct for relationships and his eye for elegant product design became the foundation stones of the journey.

Through the years, CVG jumped from one academic problem to another: flying robots, football-playing robots, underwater vehicles. The thrill was real. "We felt like kids in a toy store."

One night, still in torn hostel T-shirts and slippers, the small group sat on the pavement outside CFI. The conversation turned heavy. They had watched seniors pour years into robotics, only to graduate into jobs far from tech. Was this all just a hobby? Should they keep building toys, or start solving real-world problems?

Over the next months, they began visiting manufacturing plants in search of harder problems. Professors Mahesh and Krishnan noticed them at the CFI open house, a display of an augmented-reality T-Rex and Captain America. The professors believed in them and introduced the group to industries approaching IITM for help.

Kids in a toy store

REAL-WORLD PROBLEMS, MOSQUITOES, AND 25,000 VOLTS

Professors Mahesh and Krishnan wanted the group to try something real. In November 2012, they pointed them to the Indian Railways' overhead equipment inspection.

Inside the inspection car, officers explained the stakes: red marks at ten, twenty, and thirty meters; a misalignment that could snap a 25,000-volt line. One mistake could derail a train.

Back in the hostel, the team stacked beds to mimic gantry height, painted reflective strips, taped and re-taped sensors, and built a wire-mesh cage to shield their Kinect. Hacks – because that was all they had.

Trials happened at midnight, when the line went clear. KV, Kishore, Kedar, and the juniors – Hari, Nikhil, Prasanna, and Abhinav – climbed onto the car in T-shirts and slippers. Mosquitoes feasted on them, the coils they carried useless. The shorthand for those nights became milk-and-biscuit breaks at the station, a quick pat for a stray dog, then back onto the car.

One night, the maintenance lead studied their latest output. A task that normally required three people and a whole night now took a few hours and one person. Relief spread across his face. In that moment, code turned into contribution. The exhilaration wasn't cleverness; it was usefulness. Those mosquito-ridden nights gave the team something competitions never could – a direct line from work to the lives it touched.

Assignments followed with ITC, MRF, and others. To keep costs low, they slept on friends' floors, then returned to campus to draft proposals with their professors. The technology problems themselves were usually solved in under eight weeks, but the proposals dragged on for six months or more. The automation systems would pay for themselves within three to six months, but the slow sales process blunted momentum.

Frustration peaked. They wanted to build something that bypassed proposals entirely. The idea stuck: a consumer photo search app where anyone could instantly find the picture they wanted. It combined some of the best AI research of that time with a universal problem.

A Bigger Ask

Kedar and Vignesh flew to the U.S. to raise $50,000 through Kickstarter, while Kishore held the team in India together. Unsure the campaign would work, they decided to meet IITM alumni in person, hoping for $5,000 checks.

The first meeting in New York was with Sharat Potharaju of Uniqode. He told them bluntly: ditch the small target, go to the Bay Area, and raise $300,000 in real venture money. It sounded absurd – their total spend to date, including flights, wasn't even $10,000. "What will we do with so much money?" they asked. "You will figure it out," Sharat said.

In San Francisco, they pitched angels and VCs. Seshan Rammohan (IITM '60s) shepherded introductions. They stayed with Kedar's cousin Manish – nights spent fixing decks, websites, demos; days filled with meetings. Deepali, their sister-in-law, saw them waiting haplessly at bus stops and began ferrying them to meetings whenever she could.

Persistence met luck at NEA. Over three back-to-back meetings in three days, the conversations deepened. On August 14, 2014, an email arrived: NEA would write a $500,000 check. Other investors joined. The round closed at $700,000. Suddenly, HyperVerge was in business.

NAMING THE DREAM

By late 2013, the experiments were piling up: biscuit inspections at ITC, weld checks at factories, overhead line inspections for the Railways. Then came a serious proposal, a purchase order worth lakhs. To execute it, they needed to register a company.

One October night, the urgency spilled into a spreadsheet. Between 9:32 and 10:53 p.m., names appeared and vanished. MAWOBE, Make the World a Better Place. PLINO, Fighting for Love and Innovation. Universal Innovation. Most of the options drew groans or laughter. The debates stretched on. Kishore eventually dozed off under the desk while KV and Kedar kept circling. At some point, stubbornness to finish mattered more than fatigue.

Then KV quipped: "HyperVerge."

Kedar looked up. "What's HyperVerge?"

"Verge is limit. Hyper is beyond. Beyond the limit," KV said.

The word carried something angular, restless. It embodied their spirit – always trying to go beyond what they knew, what they had, what seemed possible.

On December 29, 2013, HyperVerge was incorporated.

LOOPS OF FAILURE

HyperVerge lurched through pivot after pivot. Industrial automation. A photo search engine. A photo-sharing app. Even a two-week sprint on an education product. Each idea gave a burst of hope; each ended in another dead end. The team was exhausted.

Sai would later call those pre-PMF years the hardest of his life: “We were going nowhere with our lives, even as we worked as hard as we could. It completely broke me. I was driven by fear of failure, and forced to bring in optimism. Maybe it was survival instinct, but it rubbed off from the others around me.”

Kishore remembered it differently, but no less painfully: “We hit what we thought was rock bottom, only to find a deeper low the very next week, and then again after that.” Failure, he learned, has no floor.

By the end of 2016, HyperVerge had six months of runway left. No product-market fit. The choices narrowed: shut down or find a way to survive.

For three long nights, the team sat in the IKP pantry and argued it through. The question scrawled on a Post-It stared back at them: If money, society, and expectations are kept aside, what do we truly want to make happen in this world?

Education, healthcare, rural employment – passions varied, but one thread ran common. Everyone wanted to work on fundamental problems. Not perception problems that gave a sugar rush of satisfaction, like a new shirt or another scroll through an app. Fundamental problems were different: they didn't always feel good in the moment, but they could transform lives – like yoga, healthcare, or education.

Yet intent alone was not enough. In conversations with early investor and confidant Venky Harinarayan, the team heard a truth that stung. “You guys have great intent. But startups cannot work on fundamental problems. Fundamental problems need decades. If you worked on education for a year, you may not even change one school in Bangalore. With six months' cash left, there is no way to do it.”

The words hit hard. The team heard the logic, but could not digest it. Instead, the question only deepened: what would it take for HyperVerge to survive at least a decade?

THE ZOHO TOUCH

As the team searched for an anchor, they found Sridhar Vembu of Zoho, an IIT Madras connection who spoke from his experience. Reading their email from the U.S., Sridhar called at 2 a.m. His advice was blunt: If you want lasting impact, first learn to stand on your own feet. Become profitable. Aim for half a million this year – two customers, $250,000 each.

Zoho itself was proof. Bootstrapped to more than $500 million in revenue back then, profitable, and quietly running a parallel contribution engine through Zoho Schools. In Chennai, the HyperVerge founders saw this up close. One engineer had studied only until Class 12, his family running a cycle-repair shop. At Zoho, he was building machine learning systems. That reality hit hard. "It brought tears to our eyes," the founders recalled. "If we have one life, this is the kind of work we want to do."

Sridhar had mentioned, almost casually, that Zoho could be one of those customers. Kedar and team followed up. When asked what it would cost, they shot back: "$250,000." Sridhar and Sailesh Kumar Davey laughed at the audacity, but still signed a six-month project for $125,000. It was the first revenue HyperVerge ever earned.

That evening there were two cakes. One in the Bangalore office. Another sent to a budget Delhi hotel where Kishore and KV were staying. White frosting, rough lettering, big grins. Small celebration. Giant step.

In the span of a year, they ran eight pilots, insurance documents, ATM cameras, time-attendance systems, geospatial imagery, iron and steel plants, even golf ball manufacturing. Each was survival, not glamor.

One of the first calls they made for help was to their mentor Swaminathan ("Swami"), an ex-Citibanker with a strong financial services network. Swami and Praveen found an opening in Vietnam. Kalidas Ghose, CEO of FE Credit, saw how HyperVerge's technologies could unify onboarding. Praveen, Sai, and the team camped in Vietnam for months to deliver. FE Credit became HyperVerge's first million-dollar customer.

From that foothold, HyperVerge found a product that opened doors to over a hundred enterprises. In the years to come, those doors would lead to more than a billion customers onboarded worldwide.

In 2017, a Zoho contract and a modest cake marked HyperVerge's first real proof of survival.

THE CONSCIOUS ENTERPRISE

By 2018, HyperVerge had money in the bank for the first time. The Delhi cake had been cut, invoices were going out, and the company was no longer on the brink.

A quieter shift began inside. The team realized that to create something conscious – and to create joy for others – they had to be joyful themselves. Kedar and Praveen deepened their spiritual journeys. Vignesh began attending Vipassana retreats and nudged Kishore and others to learn it. In the Bangalore office, they set up a small meditation room. Swami introduced them to Cheenu, who started coaching them. Slowly, the atmosphere changed – from compulsiveness to a little more awareness each day.

By 2019, HyperVerge had moved from default dead to default alive. The next question surfaced: how would they now contribute?

The core business itself – identity verification – already mattered. Every time the cost of a transaction fell, more people gained access to financial services. A ₹3,000 loan was unviable if processing cost ₹500. But if the cost dropped to ₹50, it worked. AI-powered digital onboarding wasn't just efficiency; it gave millions access to credit. And yet, the team began to look for something even more transformative.

GRADUATION VOICES

In 2020, the team set aside a budget for fundamental problems. Around that time, Gayathri – an IITM junior they considered one of the smartest they had met – knocked on their door. After Goldman Sachs, she had felt a calling: she wanted her work to change people's lives more directly.

She joined HyperVerge, tested ideas like a startup founder, and helped the team narrow down. One problem struck close to everyone's heart: training students from disadvantaged families for jobs that could break cycles of poverty.

The first batch was small: twenty-three students from families earning less than ₹2 lakh a year. The goal was precise – can they be trained for jobs averaging ₹5 lakh in the software industry? The academy built an end-to-end path: technical foundations, communication, résumés, interviews, each learner walked to the finish line.

The stories still ripple. Rani, eldest of four sisters, her father selling fruits on the roadside: "When HyperVerge chose me, I received not just training – but belief." She began with a ₹2.4 LPA offer and now earns over ₹10 LPA. Another learner said: "I rejected a low-paying job. Because of HVA, I have the confidence I deserve better."

One offer letter could transform a household. A daughter from a ₹2 lakh family stepping into a ₹5 lakh job meant health insurance where worry once sat; a bank loan replacing the moneylender's number; a ₹500 SIP starting quietly. Dignity, and better sleep.

The ripple extended further. The first graduate became the proof-point for siblings and cousins: can be done.

Gayathri built the academy not with hired trainers, but with volunteers. Engineers spent an hour a day on technical skills. Others coached communication. The team even built Sensai, a learning companion that personalized practice, flagged learners at risk, and stretched fast movers.

By 2024, the academy had helped eighty families break out of generational poverty. In 2025, it received 2,500+ applications, aiming to help 150 families in a single year. Just as business compounds, so too does contribution.

SEEDS FOR TOMORROW

By then, success meant something narrower: economic engines that earned cleanly, contribution engines that built meaning, and people who could hold both. If done well, HyperVerge would outlast them – not as a valuation, but as a vessel for human beings capable of carrying intent forward.

A decade in, the focus inside had shifted. Exits, valuations, and series letters had lost their pull. What remained was the harder question of continuity: what would truly outlast them?

Two engines began to take shape. The first was economic. Projects had to stand on their own – priced, delivered, collected. Kedar described the search for moats with precision: "Network effects for LinkedIn, Meta, Google. Switching costs for AWS, Azure, defense companies. Exclusive licenses for telcos, mining, oil and gas. At HyperVerge, we have always been in search of these moats because our mission needs it. We strive hard every day to find them." Clean economics was not an abstraction; without it, the rest could not stand.

The second was contribution. HyperVerge Academy became its face – training students from under-resourced backgrounds in software and communication, placing them into jobs that could reset entire families. Gayathri carried this engine forward with the tenacity of a founder, ensuring that contribution was not a parallel initiative but a compounding practice.

The team observed that the economic engine provides patient capital to the contribution engine, and the contribution engine provides purpose back to the economic engine.

The metaphors revealed what the numbers could not. Sai borrowed one from Cheenu: "When a seed is sown today, it provides the shade for someone else tomorrow. The action of sowing still succeeds, and it need not necessarily be reaped by the sower."

At the academy, this endurance took the form of learning facilitators – guides who stayed with each student from entry to placement. They were, in effect, co-founders of each learner's journey, holding them steady through doubt or fatigue so that no one dropped out halfway.

For Kedar, it sharpened into a principle: "To make the mission of HyperVerge happen, we require, above all, conscious human beings. Office buildings, products, money in the bank can never become conscious. The only thing that can become conscious is a human being."

Praveen called his arc "from something to nothing – the joy of dissolving."

Vignesh's words were plainer: "Being useful."

Kishore described contribution as "bringing together people in an environment that sounds like a mildly chaotic ashram so that they can go about building conscious, contributing organizations in the world."

Sai added his own metaphors of role: sculptor, delivery person, jigsaw piece. "It's as much their story as mine," he said of the backbone – Hari, Nikhil, Adarsh, Rajath, Sanchit, Anusha. They had stayed more than a decade, not as footnotes but as the institution itself.

Even today, there is a relentless search for new products that will help build a sturdier economic engine. At the same time, there is a search for ways to take the contribution engine to thousands more people.

The mission endures: to make happen a conscious business that outlasts its founders – and to inspire a hundred leaders to do the same.

WHAT ENDURES

At the end, HyperVerge is not one voice, but many. Each founder carries a different note – failure, dissolving, unity, surrender, usefulness – and together they form the tune that has held across a decade.

Kishore speaks of failure until the word bends into something else: "Over these years, my relationship with failure has changed completely... We hit what we thought was rock bottom, only to find a deeper low the very next week, and then again after that."

"If everything we've built ended tomorrow...it would still be a journey worth having lived."

Praveen carries the journey inward:

"By the grace of my Guru, one day I experientially realized that I am but a Witness and not the mind or body... The question of 'What is my purpose here?' dissolved."

His measure of success is plain: "If a person gives more than what he takes, while being situated in happiness, I call it a success."

Or in fewer words: "From something to nothing – the joy of dissolving."

Sai remembers the hardest stretch, the years of searching without direction:

"The pre-PMF days completely broke me... I was forced to bring in more optimism."

His anchor is simple: "Unity is strength."

And he names the invisible scaffolding that held the company upright: "The mentors, the IITM ecosystem, the SaaS community, Swami and Cheenu, our families, Hari, Nikhil, Adarsh, Rajath, Sanchit, Anusha...it's as much their story as it's mine."

Kedar calls endurance surrender:

"Earlier I would ask myself, am I willing to die for this mission? Later I realized, falling dead is easy. But...we should be willing to live and strive every day to make it happen."

His prayer remains unchanged: "My only prayer to my Guru has been – make something useful out of our lives."

Vignesh ties it back to the first night usefulness became real:

"Those five hundred lines of code might not have been much for me – but in another person's life it could create a huge world of impact."

He learned to separate "perception problems" from "fundamental problems," and titles his own arc with two words: "Being useful."

Together, these voices do not converge into one, but they circle the same question first written on a Post-It in 2016: "If money and societal conditioning weren't a problem, what would you do with the rest of your life? What would you want to invest your life energy into?"

The answers are not identical. One speaks of grace, another of dissolving, another of unity, another of surrender, another of usefulness. But heard together, they form a single commitment: to build an enterprise where people – not products, not valuations – become the compounding engine.

HyperVerge remains unfinished. So do they.

EPILOGUE

Ten Truths, Two Journeys

By Subrata Mitra

Looking back on six decades of life – and decades of walking alongside founders – I don't see straight lines. I see endurance. I see people who were knocked down, written off, even broken. Yet they found a way to stand again.

This book is filled with such stories. They are not fairy tales of sudden brilliance. They are accounts of men and women who were scarred and still kept going. In their struggles, I recognize patterns. In their persistence, I find lessons that are not about companies alone, but about life itself.

As I turn sixty, I carry forward ten truths. They are not commandments in stone. They are reminders carved from the journeys I've witnessed.

TEN TRUTHS THAT ENDURE

1. Roots Matter.

What you carry from childhood – values, scars, small acts of dignity – lasts longer than any venture. Mukesh Prasad Singh carried his father's struggles in Bokaro and Nirala's Bhikshuk like a backbone. That memory of survival shaped every choice that followed.

2. Build on Complements.

No founder makes it alone. The strongest teams are not mirrors but counterweights. At Ninjacart, KK's relentlessness found balance in Thiru's vision. At BlueStone, Gaurav Singh Kushwaha's drive was anchored by teams that steadied product and execution. At Uniqode, Sharat's sharp commercial sense found its counterweight in Ravi's product mind. Complementary strength is stability.

3. From Generalist to Specialist.

Founders thrive in ambiguity at the start, but scale demands letting go. Sanjay Nayak began as an engineer and salesman rolled into one. Tejas reached the world stage only when he trusted specialists to carry what he once held.

4. Keep Growing.

A company cannot outgrow its founders. Aneesh Reddy's Vipassana retreat forced him to confront ego and conflict. That shift didn't just change him; it saved Capillary.

5. Seek Stillness.

Noise surrounds every crisis. Clarity comes only in silence. For Aneesh, it was Vipassana. For KK, it was midnight runs through Bangalore when Ninjacart was on the brink. Stillness steadies the hand when the storm refuses to end.

6. Stay Stoic.

Success and failure are both impostors. Gaurav Singh Kushwaha was written off after his first collapse. He stayed steady, endured the whispers, and built BlueStone. Stoicism is not detachment; it is the refusal to let labels define you.

7. Control the Inputs.

The outcome is never fully yours. Effort is. Akash Gupta rebuilt GreyOrange by focusing on throughput, cashflow, and discipline, even as markets turned against him. He prepared so luck could find him ready.

8. Find Mentors.

The right guides alter your path. For Sharat and Ravi, even voices at home – Sowmya and Vidya – kept them alive when belief faltered. Mentorship is not advice alone; it is presence.

9. Remain Not-Out.

Endurance matters more than style. Kishore Natarajan and the HyperVerge founders stayed at the crease through failed projects, waiting until something clicked. Survival is often the only strategy you need.

10. Make the Road Joyful.

The journey is long, and grit without joy collapses. KK kept his team laughing, sharing meals, staying human even in chaos. Joy is not a distraction – it is fuel for the road ahead.

These truths were forged in the fire of entrepreneurial struggle. But wisdom does not live only in boardrooms or crisis meetings. A few years ago, I went back to Don Bosco, Kolkata – my old school – to speak to a hall full of restless eighth graders. I didn't want to give them a lecture. I wanted to slip into their pockets ten things I wished someone had given me when I was their age.

WHAT I TOLD A BUNCH OF EIGHTH GRADERS

1. Backbenchers can win big.

Till Class 5, I was a backbencher. Nobody was betting on me. Then subjects split, clarity came, and everything changed. Don't count yourself out too early.

2. If nobody answers your call, walk alone.

Tagore's "Ekla cholo re" has carried me through stretches of solitude. Learn to walk solo until you find companions you trust deeply.

3. Go to school to make friends.

Books are online. Friendship isn't. The people who stay and argue with you, even when you're wrong, will shape you.

4. Find your unique skills, and double down.

Don't waste time dragging yourself from the fortieth percentile to the fiftieth – it won't create much value. Push your edge from eighty to ninety-five – and build with others who cover your blind spots.

5. Control what you can. Influence what you can't. Accept the rest.

I wanted to be a professor. No school wanted me. Later, I left IBM Research without a plan. Both looked like mistakes. Both turned out to be gifts. Randomness has more to say than we admit.

6. Be yourself, always.

Especially in adversity. Don't copy styles. Bring your whole self into the room – it's the only way you'll last.

7. Take risks early.

Your real advantage when young is bounce-back ability. Use it before life's weight slows you.

8. Stay positive.

Adversity is rarely an end. It is usually an unmarked beginning.

9. Give more than you take.

People act in ways you won't always understand. That doesn't make them wrong or bad, just unreadable to you at that moment. Have empathy. Kindness is always underrated.

10. Have fun.

When things feel difficult, I have laughed with co-founders after setbacks. I have joked in tense board meetings and smiled at a chaiwallah on dark days. Fun doesn't solve everything, but it gets you back to a better rhythm to solve newer problems.

I doubt I taught them anything new that morning. But maybe I reminded them of what they already knew: that backbenchers can surprise, that solitude isn't failure, that joy and kindness are part of survival.

And maybe that is the circle worth closing. The founders in this book lived the same truths I once shared with schoolchildren. Whether you are chasing marks or chasing markets, whether you are staring at exams or staring at failure, the lessons remain the same:

Hold steady.
Remain not-out.
Laugh when you can.

When you realize you have less and less time, you start focusing on the more and more important things.

ABOUT THE AUTHORS

Subrata Mitra is a founder-turned-venture-capitalist and a partner at Accel. He began his career as a computer scientist and entrepreneur, co-founding Firewhite in 1999, one of the earliest attempts at enterprise software for handheld devices. In 2004, he helped start Erasmic Venture Fund, which became Accel's India practice in 2008.

Pankaj Mishra, journalist and co-founder of FactorDaily, has spent over two decades telling stories that create deep, personal connections. His *Outliers* podcast began in sound and traveled into words, shaping his book *Against the Grain*.

HarperCollins *Publishers* India

At HarperCollins India, we believe in telling the best stories and finding the widest readership for our books in every format possible. We started publishing in 1992; a great deal has changed since then, but what has remained constant is the passion with which our authors write their books, the love with which readers receive them, and the sheer joy and excitement that we as publishers feel in being a part of the publishing process.

Over the years, we've had the pleasure of publishing some of the finest writing from the subcontinent and around the world, including several award-winning titles and some of the biggest bestsellers in India's publishing history. But nothing has meant more to us than the fact that millions of people have read the books we published, and that somewhere, a book of ours might have made a difference.

As we look to the future, we go back to that one word—a word which has been a driving force for us all these years.

Read.